Women Like Us

Women Like Us

Learn More about Yourself
through Studies of Bible Women

MAGGIE MASON

WORD BOOKS
PUBLISHER
WACO, TEXAS

First Printing—August, 1978
Second Printing—January, 1979
Third Printing—February, 1980

ISBN 0-8499-2835-4
Library of Congress catalog card number: 78-57550
Printed in the United States of America

Contents

Introduction

The women of the Bible. They were living, feeling, learning persons. They were like us, and like people we know. Yet they lived in the context of their day.

This study guide is meant to help you know these women as they were in their own setting, to recognize the experience, the restrictions, the customs from which they spoke.

But if we stop there, we have accomplished only part of our purpose. For they also share with us a common humanity and womanhood.

They brought themselves and all they were in their encounters with God, just as we do. Knowing that helps us know them—and more important, know ourselves.

How to Use This Book

Women Like Us is designed for small-group study. A larger group will find it necessary to divide into sections to permit the closeness which these studies encourage.

Take the "At-Home Preparation" seriously, following the order of suggestions and not skipping any steps. You will miss a lot in your own process of discovery, for instance, if you let the printed story about the central character impose on your own exploration of Scripture.

A leader is implied—someone who has read more thoroughly than everyone has time to and who will keep a very elastic time-watch on the meeting. The leader, too, is a learner, a seeker, like every member of the group. Perhaps the leadership can be passed around among the group members.

Chapter 1

Eunice

A Woman Who Gave

Blessed by hindsight, it would be easy to oversimplify the story of this family in Lystra. But when it happened, real, feeling, less-than-perfect people faced real, painful decisions. The "You Are There" section will help you transplant yourself, just as you are, to Lystra. This can be a rich lesson in self-discovery.

At-Home Preparation

1) Read Acts 14:1–22; 15:36–16:5; 1 Timothy 1:18–20; 6:1–12; 2 Timothy 1:1–7; 3:14–17. (Extended reading for leaders: add 1 Corinthians 16:10–11. Use several versions and translations.)

2) Prepare your responses to "In the Lines" and "Between the Lines."

3) Read "About Eunice." Does the story help you understand her better?

4) The last section, "You are There," will be completed at the meeting.

9

Meeting Procedure

1) Compare and discuss your answers to "In the Lines" and "Between the Lines." Exchange discoveries from different versions and translations that enrich your understanding (20 minutes).

2) Discuss your reaction to the story, "About Eunice" (5 minutes).

3) If the group is larger than six, divide to discuss "You Are There" questions 1 to 4. Be sure that everyone in the smaller groups has opportunity to speak and to be listened to (30 minutes).

4) Regroup to discuss responses to questions 1 to 4 and to combine answers to question 5 (15 minutes).

In the Lines

1) Name the members of Eunice's family.

2) Where was their home?

3) Who founded the Christian church there?

4) Why is Eunice's son important in the Bible account?

5) How did Paul regard him?

Between the Lines

1) Circumcision was a religious rite required of every male Jew—usually performed when he was eight days old. What do you read into the fact that Timothy had not been circumcised?

2) From the different versions and translations of the Bible which you may have, list the different ways of expressing what the King James Version calls "unfeigned faith" (2 Tim. 1:5).

3) As a widow, Eunice may well have worked to support the family. (See next section, "About Eunice," for a discussion of her possible widowhood.) What do you discern about the relationship between Eunice and her mother, Lois?

About Eunice

Paul was returning to Lystra!

The word went out through the strong Christian church that had developed there since his first visits, some five years before. Eunice, her son Timothy, and her mother Lois were among those who planned for his return. He was bringing a man called Silas with him.

They would need a place to stay, meals, and homes large enough to contain the crowds that would come to hear them preach and teach.

If Eunice could have known the heartache that his coming was to bring!

But now, busy with preparation, she could only think about the day the three of them had first gone to hear Paul preach. Timothy was a gangling youth then—the pride and comfort of their home.

All of the Jews in Lystra had heard about Paul, the famous teacher who had become a believer in some strange sect that accepted even Gentiles. It was curiosity that brought the cautious Jews to mingle with the pagan Lystrans that gathered around Paul and Barnabas.

Eunice, Timothy, and Lois had lingered around the edge of the crowd; it wasn't appropriate that they—two women and an immature lad—should participate in the discussion. And besides, they had learned to be wary on the streets of Lystra, for this city was as explosive as it was prosperous and subject to sudden changes of mood. A friendly street could erupt with violence—particularly for the eternal misfits, the Jews. But they weren't so far away but that they saw the miracle: a man born lame was suddenly healed by a word from Paul!

While the Jews in the crowd discussed among themselves (was this man sent by God? did he speak the message of God?), the Lystrans proclaimed that Paul and Barnabas were themselves gods and set about to prepare sacrifices to them.

Eunice, Lois and Timothy hurried home, eager to put distance between themselves and what looked like trouble.

Once home, they talked over the strange sayings of Paul, and marveled at the miracle. They searched the Scriptures together, as they had always done. Timothy's father had been a Greek unschooled in the Hebrew Scriptures, so there had never been a man to lead them in their study. (Most authorities agree that Eunice was a widow. Whether or not Timothy's father was living he has no active part in the biblical account.) Nor was there a Jewish synagogue in Lystra where they could find guidance or observe the Jewish rituals. The three stood alone, clinging to their ancient faith.

This new teacher said wonderful things, but they must be careful. Then again, there was something about his words . . . Jesus . . . a savior . . . the promised Christ! Paul and Barnabas said this Jesus had done many great works. He had spoken words that could only be from God. He had been hated by the temple leaders, betrayed by a disciple, crucified by the Romans. But he had risen from the dead!

A few days later, while they still pondered these things, they heard that angry Jews from Iconium had followed Paul and Barnabas to Lystra and stirred up the people against them. The same crowd that had been intent on making them gods now stoned Paul to the death and dragged him outside the city.

In their home, grief had mingled with disappointment. More and more they were convinced that Paul spoke the truth.

Then, as if to seal their growing faith, they heard the miraculous news that Paul was not dead. Even more, he had dared to return to Lystra to encourage those who believed. Eunice's family were among those who met to hear Paul again as he appointed leaders and taught the believers. "Christians," he called them.

Supported now by others who believed, both Jews and Greeks, the two women studied the Scriptures with Timothy beside them. And the more they studied, the stronger their faith became. Their study bore fruit in Timothy. Eunice was pleased to see him, young as he was, become respected among the Christians and a leader in the church.

And now Paul was returning. A large, strong church waited to greet him. Eunice sang about her work, never dreaming of Paul's plans and how they would affect her life.

For Paul had heard of Timothy even before he reached Lystra. And when Paul said to Timothy, "Come with me! I need you!" Timothy didn't hesitate. He of course asked the blessing of his mother and grandmother. If they wavered, they remembered that Jesus, too, had called young men to follow him. They, too, had mothers and grandmothers, and some had wives and children.

Timothy was excited about the adventures ahead; Lois and Eunice were appalled at the perils, the great distances between them, the months and years that would pass before they saw him again.

Maybe if they insisted that he stay . . . maybe if they persuaded him it was his duty to care for them . . . but they let him go. And when their house echoed with loneliness, they read his letters and heard with pride of his development into a strong and trusted colaborer with Paul. Paul gave to Timothy his most delicate missions, his most arduous journeys. Timothy was appointed to pastor the large Christian community in Ephesus. Paul loved him as a son. And Timothy loved Paul as a father.

Eunice and Lois lived out their days in Lystra.

You Are There

1) You are a neighbor, also a Jew, in Lystra. From what you know about yourself, what would probably have been your response to Paul's ministry in Lystra?

_____I would have been one of his first converts.

_____I would have relied on my husband's decision.

_____I would have waited to see what most of my friends did.

_____I would have been a secret believer.

_____I would have decided against this new religion. Other—

2) Describe how you would have arrived at this decision, and the particular part of your personality, background, and experience which would have directed you.

3) Timothy, your son, came to you for advice before making his decision about whether or not to go with Paul. Knowing yourself, how would you have counseled him?

4) You are a Christian woman, also a mother, in Lystra. Paul has just left taking Timothy with him. You

want to say the right thing to Eunice after the church meeting next Lord's Day. What would you choose to say? Why?

5) "From his birth, a mother begins to train a child to get along without her." How do you feel about this statement? If you agree that it is true, describe some of the steps in this lifelong procedure. Discuss the implications of taking or not taking these steps, for both mother and child.

Chapter 2

```
┌─────────────────────────────────────────┐
│                                         │
│               Leah                      │
│                                         │
│          A Love Unreturned              │
│                                         │
└─────────────────────────────────────────┘
```

This Bible study may probe deep, unresolved feelings that extend far back into childhood; or it may reveal present, painful life situations. Let your preparation be honest and be ready to give understanding, support, and help to others.

At-Home Preparation

1) Read Genesis 29:16–30:21; 33:1–2. (Extended reading for leaders, Genesis 29–35.)

2) Prepare your responses to "In the Lines" and "Between the Lines."

3) Read "About Leah"; be prepared to comment on your reaction to the story.

4) The last section, "You Are There," will be completed at the meeting.

Meeting Procedure

1) Compare and discuss responses to "In the Lines" and "Between the Lines" (20 minutes).

2) Share impressions of the story, "About Leah" (5 minutes).

3) Each woman will work individually on "You Are There" (15 minutes).

4) If the group is larger than six, divide to discuss, "You Are There" (20 minutes).

5) Regroup for prayer, discussion (20 minutes).

In the Lines

1) How does the writer of Genesis compare Leah and Rachel?

2) What reason did Laban give for his deception of Jacob?

3) What did Leah name her six sons? Her daughter? What do their names tell you about Leah?

4) Describe the order of the procession as Jacob arranged his family for the hazardous meeting with his brother, Esau. What does this tell you about the status of the sisters?

Between the Lines

1) Which of these terms describe Leah's feeling for Jacob?

____romantic love ____admiration ____reverence _____resentment _____respect _____suspicion _____sexual attraction ____jealousy other__

2) What do you discern as the continuing relationship between the sisters?

3) Assign these characteristics as they seem to fit the two sisters. Some may fit both, some neither. Add others as they occur to you.

gentle, ambitious, vivacious, introverted, sexy, loyal, loving, obedient, wise, clever, reserved, selfish, petulant, manipulative, willful, resigned, selfish

          Rachel   *Leah*

About Leah

Leah, elder daughter of Laban, granddaughter of Nahor, was a woman to be envied. The sheik, her father, had inherited and built up immense holdings in the land of Haran. Haran was a fertile country, rich in olives, figs, grapes, barley, and wheat—not to mention the vast grasslands which supported great herds of cattle and sheep. Leah's home was furnished with the finest of tapestries; her table bore the best of food.

Along with her younger sister Rachel, Leah learned to work—but only at tasks fitting for the daughter of a sheik. The more menial chores were borne by slaves and servants.

From earliest childhood the sisters had been taught that their success and happiness lay in bearing sons to a man who would provide for them, protect them, and, if they were lucky, be kind to them and perhaps even love them.

But their position as daughters of Laban presented special problems: few of the men of Haran would aspire to marry them. Even if they were wealthy enough for Laban to consider (he was known as a grasping man), their religion would disqualify them. For though Laban had made many compromises with the religion of Haran, still his daughters must marry men of their own tribe—men who continued the worship of One God in the tradition of his grandfather, Terah, the courageous Semite who had fled the pagan influences of Ur.

And the tribe was considerably thinned since Laban's uncle Abraham and his cousin Lot had moved far to the south into Canaan.

Leah had an added disadvantage: her sister Rachel. Beautiful, vivacious, bright-eyed, lovable Rachel. The writer of Genesis does not spell out Leah's appearance, but he makes it clear that she wasn't in the running with Rachel.

Besides her lack of physical beauty, Leah was quiet, introverted. Perhaps because of her appearance, she was inclined to concentrate on her own thoughts. She seems to have learned inner discipline and strength and a completeness with herself that the outgoing Rachel didn't find necessary.

When the handsome, daring Jacob, their cousin from the south, appeared, it was love at first sight for him and his beautiful counterpart Rachel.

Who could help loving her? Certainly not Leah.

For Rachel, Jacob arranged to pay the bride-price. He was seven years working off Laban's exorbitant asking.

Leah should have been glad for her sister . . . except . . . she, too, loved Jacob. Every tender glance between Jacob and Rachel was a knife turning in her heart. And when the sisters were on their pallets in the dark of the night and Rachel bubbled over with the joy of her love, Leah wept quietly. Was there no future for her? No sons? No love?

When Laban explained to her his scheme to trick Jacob, it didn't occur to her to refuse; a daughter didn't.

And after Jacob's first fury (how it hurt her!) he settled down to the accepted lifestyle of an up-and-coming young prince with two wives, eventually two concubines, and a family that attested his virility and assured his continuity.

Leah quickly bore him four sons. Their names suggest her heartache and how deeply she loved Jacob. She loved Rachel: only once does Scripture record a quarrel, and that was when Leah's son found and brought her the potent mandrake—a sure aphrodisiac and fertility charm. But even that quarrel was quickly settled.

When Jacob thought about going back to his home country, he consulted his wives in his decision. They supported him and cast their loyalty with him against their father.

Soon after the tribe reached Shechem in Canaan, Rachel died in giving birth to her second son Benjamin. Leah now had the status of Jacob's chief wife. She followed him in still another move, this time to Hebron, where she met his aged father, Isaac. She comforted her husband in his later years.

Time to come would see her sons involved with the sons of the concubines in a plot against the favorite son Joseph, Rachel's child. Yet it was two of Leah's sons, Reuben and Judah, who persuaded the outraged brothers to spare Joseph's life, and Judah offered to stand as hostage in their brother Benjamin's stead.

Could it be that some of the patient tolerance of Leah was learned by her sons?

God counted them worthy, for Judah was the son of Jacob whom God chose to continue the royal line: Boaz, David, Jesus. And Leah's son Levi was chosen to head the priestly line of Israel.

So to Leah came the best part, after all.

You Are There

1) Leah's heartache, unreturned love, is not limited to man-woman relationships. What other relationships might this be a part of?

2) Have you ever been on the giving-losing end of such relationships? How did you feel?

_____hurt _____depressed _____rejected _____angry at my-

self ____angry at the other person ____jealous ____
stupid ____confused ____humiliated ____determined
other—

3) How did you react?
____tried harder ____hung on ____made myself
indispensable ____left in a huff ____cried ____cried
alone ____blew my top ____gave up quickly ____pre-
tended it wasn't important to me ____looked elsewhere
____ drew tighter into my self   other—

4) Did your reaction express your feelings? If not,
how did you deal with your feelings?
____took them out on someone else ____cried on a
friendly shoulder ____rejected them ____ignored them
____prayed ____submitted to the inevitable ____tried
to forget   other—

5) Answer this question in the light of your responses
to the previous questions: "If I had been Leah, I would
have—

6) I can understand Leah because:

7) Knowing Leah has taught me:

Chapter 3

Priscilla

A Gifted Woman

Have you ever thought about Priscilla—really thought about her—and her deviation from what is often considered the New Testament prototype of women in the church? This study may help you to a new understanding of women in the early church, and move you to a consideration of your own latent gifts.

At-Home Preparation

1) Read Acts 18:1–28; Romans 16:1–5; 1 Corinthians 16:19–20; 2 Timothy 4:19. (Extended reading for leaders: Acts 16:14, 40; 17:22–34; 18:1–28; 21:8, 9; Romans 16:1–16; 1 Corinthians 16:13–20; 2 Timothy 4:19.)

2) Prepare your answers to "In the Lines" and "Between the Lines."

3) Read "About Priscilla."

4) Does the story fit your own interpretation from the Scripture reading? Disagree if you like.

5) "You Are There" will be completed and discussed at the meeting.

Meeting Procedure

1) Compare and discuss responses to "In the Lines" and "Between the Lines" (15 minutes).

2) Discuss your reaction to the story, "About Priscilla" (10 minutes).

3) If the group is larger than six, divide for the "You Are There" portion. Each woman will then work individually on written responses to "You Are There" (15 minutes).

4) Each group will discuss among themselves their responses (20 minutes).

5) Regroup for discussion and prayer. Special prayer subjects: women leaders in the church, personal spiritual gifts (20 minutes).

In the Lines

1) In what three cities did Priscilla live?

2) What was her occupation?

3) By what name did her intimates know her?

4) What were the circumstances of her first meeting with Paul?

5) Why did she and her husband feel they must "expound" the way of God to Apollos?

Between the Lines

1) List at least four characteristics which describe Priscilla.

2) What evidence does Scripture give that Priscilla and Aquila were active witnesses to their faith?

3) What might have been the subject of their conversation as they worked side by side with Paul, making tents?

4) Priscilla was faced with repeated crises. Name several.

5) What did Priscilla and Aquila foresee as the result if they did not correct Apollos?

6) How did Paul feel about Priscilla? .

About Priscilla

The remarkable thing about Priscilla is that in the New Testament she is not pointed out as being remarkable. Not that she is taken for granted: the Apostle Paul regarded her with admiration and confidence, and even affection—he called her by the intimate "Prisca."

But when Luke wrote about Paul's first meeting with her and her husband Aquila in Corinth, he makes no great to-do about her working as a tentmaker. Nor does he seem particularly shocked when she joined with her husband in instructing the powerful preacher Apollos in spiritual matters.

Priscilla was a student of Scripture, which doesn't fit at all the picture we usually get of women in the early church—women who were asked to please not disturb the meeting with their questions.

However, knowing the times and knowing Priscilla, you can be sure she must have had parents who were far-seeing and wise. Jewish boys learned a self-supporting trade as a matter of course—even the scholarly Paul knew how to make a living with his hands. They were taught the Scriptures along with reading and writing, but such teaching was said to be wasted on a woman. Priscilla seems to have been raised much like her brothers. A by-product of this background was a dignity and self-confidence that made her equal to the tough demands of being a Christian in her day.

You may read into Priscilla's story a good marriage to a strong and understanding man. Their names are never mentioned separately. Sometimes his name is first, sometimes hers. Together they were driven out of Italy under the wrath of the emperor Claudius—persecuted not because they were Christians, but because they were Jews. *They* taught Apollos; the church met in *their* home. They sold their belongings, left established businesses, and at least three times moved to where a young group of Christians needed their support.

It wasn't easy to be a Christian in Corinth, or in Ephesus. Both were wealthy, bustling, cosmopolitan cities; both were also centers of idolatrous worship which made vice a religious virtue. In Corinth it was the goddess Aphrodite who called the faithful. In Ephesus it was Diana (her Greek name was Artemis), and there Christianity threatened a thriving tourist business which centered on the cult of Diana. Even worse than the opposition of the pagan community was the opposition of certain Jews in these cities.

But in both places, and before and after again in Rome, Aquila and Priscilla dared to live out and witness to their faith. Their home was open. Paul, Apollos, and later Titus and Timothy, found hospitality there. The couple opened their doors to the church, suffering the attending threats and persecution.

Scripture leaves a hole we'd like to fill. What event drew Paul to write this commendation: "They have risked their necks to save my life"? And why did the Gentiles owe Priscilla and Aquila a special debt?

Running through the brief outline of Scripture, covering about ten years' time, is a series of crises which the two faced together. The first was their expulsion from Italy. Later it was the question, should they confront the great Apollos when they felt him to be both shallow and inaccurate in his knowledge of Christ? It would have been easier to keep quiet. Should they leave Corinth with Paul? And what about returning to Rome . . . a risky business?

Their story is left unfinished. Did they live out long lives as the strength and stability of the church at Rome? Did they visit Paul when he was a prisoner there? Did they move to still another beginning church? Did they die for their faith?

Whatever the answers, we may be certain that Priscilla's faith, courage, discipline, and wisdom contributed immeasurably to the development of the early Christian church.

You Are There

1) You are Priscilla's neighbor in Corinth. You are a believer. How would you feel about her?

____envy ____hostility ____admiration ____censure ____love ____awe ____doubt ____confusion ____resentment   other__

2) Priscilla confides in you her questions about Apollos and asks your advice about whether or not to confront him. How would you have advised her?

____Apollos must know what he is doing; he is so learned, and such a great preacher!

____It isn't a woman's place to interfere—especially in spiritual matters.

____Let Aquila decide.

____You could get into trouble! Apollos is an influential man.

____If you feel sure of God's leading, go ahead. But count me out.

_____Yes, certainly, if you are sure it is right.
Other__

3) Move Priscilla up to the last quarter of the twen-
tieth century. She is in your town. Maybe a member of
your church. What places would she fill?

_____She would be president of the ladies aid.

_____She would run for election to the city council.

_____She would be president of a local feminist group.

_____She would be taking advanced classes at the local
university.

_____She would teach a kindergarten class in Sunday
school.

_____She would be elected to serve communion in our
church.

_____She would be the person everyone turned to for
comfort and counsel.

_____She would head the local March of Dimes drive.
Other__

4) Priscilla was undoubtedly a gifted woman. Do you
see any of Priscilla's gifts in yourself?

_____confidence _____leadership ability _____love of
Scripture _____decisiveness _____courage _____insight
_____hospitality _____partnership in marriage _____easy
hold on possessions other__

5) Do you recognize these gifts in other women in
your group? State some.

6) Name a woman (or several women) you know who is much like Priscilla. A man (or several).

7) The most memorable thing about Priscilla's story is:

The most surprising:

The most disturbing:

Chapter 4

Hagar
A Woman Used

Hagar. You can skim over her story if you like, but faithfully studied, she reveals a side of God's nature we don't often see. What is more, learning about Hagar may open for you some new understanding of yourself.

At-Home Preparation

1) Read Genesis 16; 21:1–21; 25:1–18. (Extended reading for leaders: add Genesis 12:1–9; 13:14–18; 15:1–6.)

2) Prepare your responses to "In the Lines" and "Between the Lines."

3) Read "About Hagar."

4) Begin to think about "You Are There." Reserve your answers for the meeting.

Meeting Procedure

1) Compare responses to "In the Lines" and "Between the Lines" (20 minutes).

2) Did "About Hagar" change some of your at-home study responses? Tell why and how (5 minutes).

3) Work individually on "You Are There" (15 minutes).

4) If the group is larger than six, divide to discuss your responses (20 minutes).

5) Regroup to compare your reactions (10 minutes).

6) In *Why Am I Afraid to Tell You Who I Am?* John Powell says, "Feelings are not moral [good or bad]." How do you respond to that statement? If you agree with him, where then does morality begin (10 minutes)?

7) Each woman will write her own personal prayer growing out of the experience of this lesson (5 minutes).

In the Lines

1) What was Hagar's status in Abram's house?

2) Twice, the Scripture records, Hagar made Sarai very angry. What brought on this anger?

3) Whom did Sarai seem to blame for Hagar's insolence?

(Note that midway through the story "Abram" becomes "Abraham" and "Sarai" becomes "Sarah.")

Between the Lines

1) What was Abraham's feeling toward Ishmael?

_____ love _____loyalty _____obligation _____pity _____re-morse _____indifference _____helplessness _____frustration _____disinterest _____responsibility   other__

2) Why, in your opinion, did Abraham send away all his sons except Isaac (Gen. 25)?

_____It was the custom of the day.

_____He didn't want in-family strife to threaten Isaac's position.

_____He truly loved only Sarah, Isaac's mother.

_____There wasn't enough inheritance to provide for all his other children.

Other__

3) How do you account for Ishmael's presence at Abraham's burial?

_____He was trying to win points with Isaac.

_____He loved his father.

_____Isaac knew his position was secure; he did not feel threatened by Ishmael.

_____Isaac was a compassionate man who understood Ishmael's affection for their father.

Other__

4) Why do you think God showed mercy to Hagar and her son?

_____He pitied her.

_____Ishmael, too, was Abraham's seed.

_____He had plans for the Arabians who would descend from Ishmael.

_____Hagar trusted God.

Other__

5) How do you feel about Hagar?
____pity ____admiration ____contempt ____affection
____anger ____impatience ____sympathy ____liking
____scorn other__

Why?

6) How do you feel about Sarah?
____respect ____confusion ____surprise ____suspicion
____disappointment ____confidence ____envy ____
like ____dislike other__

Why?

7) Contrast Hagar's reaction to her two exiles from Abraham's house. List the terms in the incident where they seem to fit.

proud, self-reliant, tense, anguished, despairing, helpless, angry, rebellious, trusting, hopeless, confused, defeated.

In Genesis 16   *In Genesis 21*

8) Of the following characteristics, which were Hagar's strengths (s)? Which her weaknesses (w)? Which were absent (a)?
____faith ____piety ____spunk ____patience ____sim-

plicity ____pride ____obedience ____self-reliance ____
rebellion ____ambition ____determination ____
loyalty ____courage ____naïveté others__

About Hagar

You haven't heard much about her. But when you read
her story, you see her as a tragic figure. You deplore her
tactlessness, you admire her spunk. You speculate on the
undescribed years of sharing a household with the domi-
neering Sarah. You weep at her son's anguish. You are
ambivalent as to whose side you are on—for you're not
at all sure who are the good guys and who the bad.

It's all very well, from the safe perspective of thirty-
five hundred years, to see "God's purpose" accomplished
in the banishment of Hagar and Ishmael. But thirty-five
hundred years ago there was flesh that burned and spirit
that suffered.

. . . and a God who saw it all. Sure, he had a plan. "In
Isaac will thy seed be called." But he also cared for the
helpless victim of man's faithlessness and depraved non-
caring.

God moved to help Hagar—not in response to her
faith, for there is no evidence that she had any acquain-
tance with Abram's God. God moved in to care for her in
response to a cry of anguish. Hagar wasn't even sure who
he was—so she gave him a name of her own inventing:
"Thou God seest me."

From our time and place, it is impossible to understand the Sarah-Hagar-Abraham triangle. The customs
of the times that seem to us immoral and savage were a

way of life in patriarchal days. God had such a lot of work to do with the human race!

Both Sarah and Hagar are reacting to a position of powerlessness—Hagar of course far down the ladder from Sarah. Sarah wheedled, threatened, manipulated, blamed, lashed out cruelly. Tactless Hagar (she must have been very young) failed miserably in trying to take advantage of a slight elevation in her position. She was forced into submission by the basic need to survive and because of her love for her son. Then there was this strange and wonderful God who had made her strange and wonderful promises in her time of trouble.

We ask something almost impossible of ourselves in even trying to understand. But such a situation was not remarkable in patriarchal days.

Sarah—strong-willed, intelligent, ambitious, frustrated —resorted to the worst of methods.

As far Hagar, an Egyptian slave girl, we have a hard time conceiving the humiliation of being given to a man as a breeding animal, or understanding Abram's passion-less impregnating. Hagar saw it as an opportunity, her only opportunity, to wrench herself out of her position. Though her bragging and derision of Sarai was unwise, it is understandable from Hagar's point of view. She had precious little to brag about.

Her desperation, her grief for her son—certainly multiplied by the utter hopelessness of her own position without him—bring home a human drama that, though most incomparable with our own, still carries human qualities common to all.

You and I may not approve of Sarah's methods—but we can feel with her the reasons why she did as she did.

We may not admire Hagar's attitude, but as mothers, as women, we can feel a deep sympathy. For both women, their lack of real self-determination drew out the worst in them.

Hagar's son and his descendants survived to become a burr under the saddle for the descendants of Isaac. Yet a Hagarite was appointed to an important position in King David's administration. They eventually populated a large section of the Arabian peninsula. We know them today as Arabs.

You Are There

1) God obviously responded to Hagar's plight, even though she didn't know him. What do you make of that?

2) Have you ever felt that you, like Hagar, were taken for granted, taken advantage of? How did you react?

_____like Hagar in chapter 16

_____like Hagar in chapter 21

_____lashed out angrily

_____turned sly, manipulative

_____resigned myself to it as my "cross"

_____forgave, forgot

_____laughed it off

_____ignored it

_____brooded about it

_____pouted

_____ran away

other __

3) Have you ever felt you were the victim of unjust treatment?

____On the job?

____As a member of a family group?

____As a wife?

____In your church?

____Among neighbors?

What were your feelings in response? ____anger ____ outrage ____frustration ____vindictiveness ____disbelief ____helplessness ____puzzlement ____patience ____forgiveness ____submission ____resignation ____ depression ____hurt other__

4) How did you express your feelings?

5) How did you feel about your feelings?

____good ____disappointed in myself ____ashamed ____satisfaction ____peace ____guilt other__

6) How can a Christian woman deal with anger? Frustration? Hurt? Other negative feelings?

Chapter 5

Elisabeth
The Supporter

Elisabeth would seem to have only a bit part in the magnificent drama of Scripture. Her appearance is brief, her lines few. But she is unforgettable for she left behind her a lasting example of sensitivity, faith, and vision. Your study of Elisabeth may remind you of people like her. Or you may see in her something of yourself.

At-Home Preparation

1) Read Luke 1:5–80; Malachi 1:6–10. (Extended reading for leaders: Luke 1; 7:19–29; John 3:22–36; 1 Chronicles 24:10; Malachi 1:6–2:9.)

2) Prepare your responses to "In the Lines" and "Between the Lines."

3) Read "About Elisabeth."

4) Prepare your responses to "You Are There," questions 1 to 3 only.

Meeting Procedure

1) Compare and discuss responses to "In the Lines"

and "Between the Lines" (20 minutes).

2) Discuss your reaction to "About Elisabeth" (5 minutes).

3) If your group is larger than six, divide to discuss your responses to "You Are There," questions 1 to 3 (10 minutes).

4) "You Are There," questions 4 to 7. Work individually. Then follow suggestions in question 8 (30 minutes).

5) Regroup if you feel inclined to, or follow the Spirit's leading of the moment.

In the Lines

1) Describe briefly the main characters in the story: their ancestry, their position, their character, their home.

2) What message did the angel bring to Zacharias?

3) Why did Zacharias doubt the angel?

4) What was Elisabeth's kinship to Mary?

5) What evidence told Elisabeth that Mary, too, had conceived, and that her child was the Son of God?

Between the Lines

1) How was Zacharias different from most priests of his day?

2) From your reading of Scripture, describe the mood of this couple as they prepared for Zacharias to take his turn in the Temple service.

3) The angel told Zacharias that their child would be what was known as a Nazarite. Such a person, man or woman, took special vows—usually for a specific period of time—that made of their person essentially a sacrifice to the Lord. (Read Numbers 6:1–8, if you are interested.) In all of Bible history, Zacharias knew of only two persons who had been "Nazarites from the womb"— set apart by God, endowed by the Holy Spirit before birth (Samson, Judges 13:5; and Samuel, 1 Samuel 1:9–30). What, then, must have been Zacharias's and Elisabeth's feelings as they knew that their son would be so set apart?

4) Try to feel with Elisabeth her emotions, her state of mind, as she waited out the first crucial months of her pregnancy. Set down some of your ideas here.

5) What do you discern as to the relationship between Elisabeth and Mary—besides their being cousins?

6) Why did Mary hurry to Elisabeth?

7) Knowing Elisabeth, what could she do for Mary?

8) We are not told by Scripture, but what do you think was the nature of John's upbringing?

About Elisabeth

The priestly line in Israel began with Aaron and his two sons. By New Testament times, the family line had grown far beyond the proportion of males needed as priests, so for the most part the priests earned their living at ordinary occupations and appeared at the Temple to perform their duties only as names were drawn, by lot, to indicate their turn. As a matter of fact, many genealogies had been lost during the time of their dispersion, and only those who could present unquestioned relationship to Aaron were acknowledged priests.

Zacharias was one such. His indisputable lineage was important to the Gospel writer Luke. His wife, Elisabeth, also traced her ancestry through the priestly line.

They lived in the hill country of Judea. Luke says simply that "they were both righteous before God, walking in all the ordinances of the Lord blameless."

This description—which from our point in time seems to be what you would expect of a priest—was far from ordinary. Malachi described the priesthood as corrupt, selfish, profane. At the best, their service was often mechanical, giving little thought to the sacred symbols they offered and the sanctity of the place where they worshiped.

All of this is said to emphasize the devotion, the dedication, the God-awareness of this unusual couple, Zacharias and Elisabeth.

As the story opens, they are both well up in years, bearing together the loneliness and stigma of being childless.

Can you see her? Elisabeth, past middle age, staunch in her devotion, setting an example of piety and godliness, bearing the burden of her childlessness, receiving her share of the curiously mixed reverence and disdain with which most of Israel regarded their priests.

Among her relatives was a young girl, Mary, who lived in Nazareth in Galilee, three days' journey to the north.

In spite of the difference in their ages, the two shared an affinity that enriched them both.

Came the time when Zacharias's name was drawn, and it was his turn to travel to Jerusalem and perform his priestly role. With what excitement did Elisabeth prepare him for his journey! With what searching of soul did they anticipate the great experience of approaching God in the Most Holy Place!

Then, a week or so later, Zacharias returned home, unable to speak and vastly changed. He communicated as best he could in writing and gesture about the vision and the voice he had witnessed in the Temple. And Elisabeth believed. Her conception shortly thereafter was reason for the greatest rejoicing. She secluded herself for five months, recognizing the vital nature of her role in bringing a special child into the world and, it may be, protecting herself and her child from complications which might follow this late-in-life pregnancy.

Then Luke switches scenes. You are moved to a time about six months ahead, and to a town in Galilee. There Elisabeth's young cousin, Mary, was also visited by an angel who announced that she, although a virgin, would be the mother of the Son of God.

Her calm resignation (Luke 1:38) isn't quite all the story. She was understandably excited, disturbed, puzzled, frightened—and she had reason to be. Where did she go for help? Her first thought—Elisabeth. And when Elisabeth rose to meet her and Mary saw the burden of child that her older cousin carried, she was amazed at this double miracle.

Elisabeth? Before Mary had a chance to tell her of her own pregnancy, Elisabeth knew. The Holy Spirit filled her, and in words that only a prophet could have spoken she announced Mary as the "mother of my Lord."

Has ever artist or musician succeeded in capturing this moment—surely one of the most poignant, powerful, and beautiful in all of history—as the two women embraced, the Holy Spirit not only filling them but seeming literally to glow and dance about them with the joy of that moment in time?

Mary, hearing her own vision verified, broke out into one of the most beautiful songs in all of Scripture, which we know today as the "Magnificat."

Here Scripture draws the curtain, almost as if the scene were too intimate for intrusion. We only know that Mary stayed with Elisabeth three months.

Maybe Mary had in mind to hide there indefinitely. *How* could she face the accusing stares of the people in her home town, now that her pregnancy was becoming obvious? Most terrible of all, how could she face Joseph, whom she dearly loved and who loved and trusted her?

What confidence, what strength the older woman must have given! Incomparable encouragement, godly trust, insight into the plan and working of God—these Elisabeth had to give, to share with a teenage girl entrusted with so holy a burden.

They pored over Scripture, finding there further substantiation of their place in the plan of salvation. Elisabeth, from her maturity and long walk with God, gave Mary the confident courage she needed to return to Nazareth.

Came Elisabeth's time to deliver, and her husky son, "filled with the Holy Ghost from his mother's womb," saw the light of day.

"His name is John" ("Jehovah had mercy"), Elisabeth insisted when others would have called him after his father. "His name is John," Zacharias repeated, writing his message. So the culmination of God's time was begun, and in celebration God restored Zacharias's voice. His first words were yet another song of praise—the third in this one chapter of Luke's Gospel.

Elisabeth and Zacharias now fade into the background. We only know that their son John lived out the fulfillment of the angel's prophecy. We can surmise, however, that in anticipation of this, Elisabeth and Zarcharias devoted their full love and devotion to his training.

For when John emerged, he was ready to be "the prophet of the Highest," going, like Elijah, to prepare the people for the coming of his cousin, the Messiah. Jesus said of him, "Among those that are born of women there is not a greater prophet than John the Baptist" (Luke 7:28).

Elisabeth and Zacharias probably did not live to see their son's ministry. They joined the multitude of those before them who received the promise only through faith, but without whom God could not have worked his plan.

You Are There

1) Can you think of someone you know who is much like Elisabeth? In searching your mind for this person, what characteristics do you look for in order to parallel her?

2) Can you picture yourself in Elisabeth's role—just supposing you had the faith and strength Scripture attributes to her—hearing a message such as Zacharias brought when he returned from his service in the Temple? How would you react?

3) Although all four Gospel writers describe the ministry of John the Baptist, only Luke reveals this intimate story. What does this tell you about Luke?

(Please note that the following questions are to be considered separately. See direction 4 under "Meeting Procedure.")

4) The young Mary obviously felt the need for human support. Have you known such time? Where did you turn?

5) Have there been times when you very much needed such a person, and you had no one?

6) Have you experienced a turn in being an "Elisabeth"?

7) Can you identify this Bible study group as often

becoming a "Mary and Elisabeth" experience? Explain.

8) You will have worked alone on questions 4 to 7 above. As you finish your work, close yourself in to meditation and private prayer. Begin by visualizing the sacred scene, the meeting of Elisabeth and Mary. Pray for yourself, that you may recognize both your "Mary" and your "Elisabeth" role and God's plan for human sharing.

Chapter 6

Abigail

A Woman Who Knew Herself

The Bible abounds with love stories; seldom does Scripture reveal the inner workings of a disastrous marriage such as that of Nabal and Abigail. The whole scene is tense in its drama, shaking in its implications. Was Abigail right in remaining "herself"?

At-Home Preparation

1) Read 1 Samuel 25; 27:3; 30:5; 2 Samuel 2:2; 1 Chronicles 3:1. (Extended reading for leaders: 1 Samuel 25; 27:1-7; 30:1-20; 2 Samuel 2:1-4; 1 Chronicles 3:1-9.)

2) Prepare your responses to "In the Lines" and "Between the Lines."

3) Read "About Abigail."

4) "You Are There" will be completed at the meeting.

Meeting Procedure

1) Compare and discuss responses to "In the Lines" (10 minutes).

2) If the group is larger than six, divide to discuss "Between the Lines" (20 minutes).

3) Regroup: discuss "About Abigail" (5 minutes).

4) Discuss as a group, "You Are There." Take the questions in order. Be sure that everyone is heard (30 minutes).

5) Pray for wisdom and courage in facing problems that have no easy answers; pray for self-understanding (10 minutes).

In the Lines

1) Name the main characters in this drama.

2) Describe Abigail's relationship to the servants in her household. Give evidence.

3) David was grateful to Abigail. Why?

4) What future did Abigail prophesy for David?

Between the Lines

1) Agree or disagree: Abigail interceded with David because she loved her husband. Support your answer, or give alternatives.

2) Align the following list of personal characteristics under the appropriate person. Some may apply to more than one; some not at all. Add others of your own perception.

impetuous, evil, decisive, diplomatic, insulting, commanding, courageous, assertive, foolish, quick-tempered, capable, faithful, small, intemperate, devout, compassionate, open-minded, arrogant, gracious, warm-hearted, sullen, parsimonious, bold, authoritative, tactful, gentle, contemptuous, closed-minded, humble, cowardly, wise, unapproachable.

Nabal   *Abigail*   *David*

3) Describe what you think Abigail's role might have been as David's wife:

Their relationship:

Her contribution to the marriage:

Her influence on David's decisions:

Her influence on David's spiritual life:

About Abigail

It was, of course, an arranged marriage. Comments around the village expressed both pity and envy for the bright, capable, beautiful Abigail.

All in all, though, it was a desirable match. Nabal was a man of importance and influence. His holdings on the rich plateau around Carmel assured his position as a man of continuing wealth. So he hadn't the best disposition and was much older than his bride—a woman couldn't expect everything. As the wife of Nabal she would have servants, luxuries, standing in the community.

Few bothered to ask if she would be happy.

Abigail soon found her place in her husband's large household. She was, in fact, in charge—what with his long absences and drunken irresponsibility. The servants, who both feared and despised Nabal, found in Abigail a capable manager who commanded their respect and admiration.

Nabal's shortcomings were no secret: he was blatant in his evil, and his wife and servants united to protect him from himself and to protect their household from the ruin his foolishness might bring down upon them all.

Many other colorations might be read into this tragic relationship: jealousy and resentment on the part of Nabal; disillusionment and frustration on the part of Abigail; long separations, silence, anger, tension, sexual problems—a completely unhappy situation for both of them. Yet Scripture states the case simply: Abigail was "of good understanding"; Nabal was "churlish and evil."

Enter David—a political exile. King Saul, treacherous, demented, hunted David throughout the wilderness with three thousand chosen men—thrashing the brush, searching the caves, as hunters might try to flush out game. David, only a jump ahead, had a devoted volunteer bodyguard of six hundred men. They lived off the land in a manner that might be termed extortion, except that David was so well loved and had the sympathy of the people. Without their loyalty he surely would have been discovered and killed.

David and his men not only did not molest Nabal's sheepherders; they protected them from marauders. Then, as was his custom, David sent ten men to respectfully collect what he figured was his due: food for his small army.

Nabal's contemptuous reply—"Many servants nowadays run away from their masters. Shall I take my meat to feed them all?"—sparked David's short-fused temper. In a fine fury, he and four hundred men set out to destroy all of Nabal's household and holdings.

But a servant who had heard Nabal's insulting retort had already reached Abigail. As the household churned in terror and Nabal moaned in a drunken stupor, Abigail took charge. In an incredibly short time the servants loaded a caravan of asses with far more food than David had requested and started down the road toward David's camp. Abigail followed as soon as she had made herself presentable—in fact, reaching David before the pack animals did.

The dramatic scene which followed is unsurpassed in Bible history: her pleading, her prophecy, David's instant repentance of his anger and his characteristic gratitude to Abigail in that she had prevented his shedding blood and "avenging myself with mine own hand." His gracious, "Go up in peace to thine house; see, I have hearkened to thy voice and accepted thy person," sent Abigail and her servants back to deal with the drunken Nabal.

When he was sober, and Abigail told him how close they had all been to death, his years of dissipation combined with a wild fear to produce what was probably a paralytic stroke. Ten days later, he died.

David's reaction to Nabal's death was in tune with his times and not unexpected. The attraction between David and Abigail, each head and shoulders above the crowd, was instantaneous and recognized by both of them.

According to Jewish laws of inheritance, since Nabal had no sons, his fortune and land holdings went to his widow. David was of the tribe of Judah, as was Nabal, so the forbidden transfer of property between tribes was not a complicating factor.

Knowing David's preoccupation with his perilous situation and later with his responsibilities as king, in all likelihood Abigail continued to manage the estate in Carmel. But she followed David in the rough, temporary camps. She shared his danger—she was once captured. She shared his love: she was the second of eight wives. She shared his glory as the beloved King of Israel.

What was her role? Scripture does not tell us, but we may be sure it was distinctive and strong. The self-knowledge that directed her as a young woman certainly sustained her in her later years. Whatever the fortunes of life, in every situation, she would persist in being uniquely herself.

You Are There

1) Did "About Abigail" influence your answers to the "Between the Lines" questions? Explain.

2) How do you feel about Abigail's description of her husband (1 Sam. 25:25, 26)?

3) Knowing yourself, what would you probably have done in Abigail's place when faced with David's revenge?

_____as she did

_____escaped

_____organized the servants to fight

_____tried to change Nabal's mind

_____resigned myself

_____sent hostages

_____sent my most trusted servant to negotiate

_____sent gifts, but stayed at home

_____wouldn't have been able to decide

_____panicked

other__

Why?

4) How would a far-out "Ms." have adjusted to this

marriage? How would she have reacted in the crisis Abigail faced?

5) How would the "Total Woman" have adjusted to this marriage? How would she have reacted in the crisis Abigail faced?

6) How does who I see myself to be influence my reaction in time of crisis? Can a change in my self-image change my reactions? Can an understanding of myself influence the direction of my life? How can I know myself? How can we help each other to a more positive self-image?

Chapter 7

Salome

An Imperfect Woman

For all her importance to the ministry of Jesus, little is told about Salome. Mostly, she is remembered for her mistake. Only by piecing together fragments of Scripture, by searching for implications, can you find her richer identity. "In the Lines" requires this sort of study.

At-Home Preparation

1) Read Matthew 20:20–28; 27:55–56; Mark 1:19–20; 15:40–41; 16:1–8; Acts 1:12–14. (Extended reading for leaders: Matthew 20:20–28; 27:45–56; Mark 1:16–20; 15:33–16:8; Acts 1:12–2:47.)

2) Prepare your responses to "In the Lines" and "Between the Lines."

3) Read "About Salome." Does the story affect your feelings about her? Does it change your understanding of her?

4) The last section, "You Are There," will be completed at the meeting.

Meeting Procedure

1) Compare and discuss answers to "In the Lines." The composite should bring out more than any one woman has learned (10 minutes).

2) Compare and discuss answers to "Between the Lines." There may be disagreements (10 minutes).

3) Discuss your reaction to "About Salome" (5 minutes).

4) Try several versions of the drama in question 1, "You Are There" (20 minutes).

5) Each woman will work individually on the remaining "You Are There" questions (10 minutes).

6) Discuss as a group your responses to "You Are There" (20 minutes).

7) Pray together, with special attention to something you have learned about yourself from this story (15 minutes).

8) Assign each member part of the list of names found in the next lesson on Deborah in the section "You Are There." Discover the "battle" each woman was involved in, and brand her particular type of courage. Ask your public library for a book of brief biographies or a biographical dictionary. Some dictionaries list women only; that would be your best resource.

In the Lines

List at least six facts about Salome which you discovered in reading the Scripture passages.

Between the Lines

1) List several possible reasons for the disciples' anger with James and John after their mother's request.

2) Why were the disciples angry with the brothers and not their mother? What might have been their feelings toward Salome?

3) Salome and other women seem to have consistently followed and served Jesus and his disciples. Why aren't they mentioned more?

About Salome

The story of Salome, like that of many Bible women, has to be arrived at obliquely. You see her most often mirrored in her sons, the apostles James and John, or in her husband, Zebedee. Only at the cross and at the tomb is she named outright.

As the wife of Zebedee, Salome was a woman of importance. Zebedee was well known in all of Galilee. He ran a prosperous fishing business out of Capernaum, a city on the west shore of the Sea of Galilee. Fishing was the core of the economy in that area; a successful fisherman was highly respected. Not only that, but fishermen had the reputation of being devout and of observing the particulars of the Jewish law. We may well suppose that theirs was a thoroughly Jewish home where the ancient customs were kept and the sons taught the Scripture from childhood.

Salome enjoyed a fine home, servants, comforts, and prestige in the community. If she followed the pattern of many women of her day, she assisted Zebedee in his business—probably keeping the books and taking care of purchasing and sales to free her husband for the management of the boats and his hired assistants.

Zebedee and Salome had two sons, James and John, who kept the home lively—and probably the community abuzz. Robust, they were—sun-browned, hearty, impulsive. (Jesus, with fond indulgence, nicknamed them "Sons of Thunder.") They were a handful—these lively, mischievous boys, who as young men were ardent, ambitious and, we may infer, seeking a Cause.

Salome, like any mother, must have been concerned about her sons' high spirits. When they first showed interest in this young teacher from Galilee, she could only think of the dangers inherent in following some radical who might get her sons in trouble with the Romans. And when the day came that they "left their nets to follow him"—can you imagine the consternation and loneliness in the home of Zebedee and Salome?

But something won them over. Was it their sons' enthusiastic devotion? Did Jesus himself visit them? Or did they take their place among the crowd of listeners and so were themselves convinced?

However it happened, some time after their sons left, Salome, too, left Capernaum, to become one of a band of women who followed Jesus. And such was Zebedee's devotion that he let her go.

You don't hear much about these women, directly. But you know someone had to furnish the money for food for the thirteen husky men who spent three years tramping about. Someone had to buy provisions, cook meals over outdoor fires, wash trail-soiled clothes. Mark implies that it was this band of women, describing them as "ministering to Jesus" in Galilee; and Matthew says they left the familiar beauty of Galilee and followed Jesus into the desolation, danger, and hardship of Judea. (A traveling, teaching rabbi and a group of followers were not uncommon in that day, nor was the band of ministering women.)

When Jesus taught, when he preached, they were nearby. They learned, they observed, they saw the miracles, they grew in understanding and in love of this remarkable Man, and eventually recognized him as who he said he was: the Christ, the Son of God.

Came the time when the disciples, except John, fled in terror; Salome was one of the women who stayed close to Jesus on the cross, identifying herself with him, sharing his suffering, comforting his mother. She was one who hurried to the tomb on the day after the Sabbath and heard the first announcement of the resurrection.

Though the women who waited in the upper room in Jerusalem were not named, in all likelihood Salome was among them.

Salome is charged with one incident that seems to mar a picture of selfless devotion; she asked for special honors for her sons. Yet Jesus did not rebuke her but used the occasion to teach one of his greatest lessons: "Those who minister are greatest; those who serve are chief." Could there have been still another meaning to his words, speaking, as he was, in the hearing of the women who made a calling of "ministering"?

We have no record of how Salome felt after this encounter: the disciples' attention is focused on her sons. Was she hurt? Did she feel misunderstood? Embarrassed? Whatever, she stayed. She learned. She grew in love and faith.

Salome asked for a chief place for her sons. Her wish was, in fact, granted. They, with Peter, were the three whom Jesus chose as his closest companions. John was called "the beloved"; his intimacy with Christ is one of the most beautiful relationships in all of Scripture. He lived out a long lifetime of service as preacher, pastor, writer of the profound Gospel of John, three letters, and the Book of Revelation. James was the first martyr among the apostles.

You Are There

1) In Capernaum, news gets around that Salome is leaving to join the band of disciples who follow Jesus. Three village women meet at the well the next day. The first is a woman who has long been jealous of Salome and her position in the community. The second is a neighbor who has shared Salome's growing faith in the new Teacher. The third is a newcomer; she has not heard of Jesus and is in fact unaware of recent events. Choose three women from your group to enact the conversation that might have taken place. Switch roles, or choose three others to enact the scene differently. The jealous neighbor, for instance, may be noisy and talkative or sly and

undercutting. The newcomer may be a know-it-all or a shy young woman trying to make herself agreeable.

2)   You are Salome; you have followed Jesus about the countryside, given generously of your purse, served, borne hardship—and when you make what seems to you a simple request, you are turned down flat, with the implication that you didn't really know what you were asking for. How would you feel?

_____misunderstood _____angry _____humbled
_____chastened _____embarrassed _____disappointed
_____puzzled _____resentful _____unappreciated
other__

3)   How do you feel about "perfect" people?
_____I'd like them better if they weren't.
_____I admire them, but from a distance.
_____I seek them out; I want to learn from them.
_____I'm uncomfortable.
_____I'm suspicious; I smell a phony.
_____I feel guilty; I should be more like them.
other__

4)   There's something about Salome's mistake that:
_____irritates me: she should have known better.
_____humbles me: I think I'd have left and gone home.
_____embarrasses me: Christians shouldn't be self-seek-
      ing.
_____embarrasses me: women shouldn't be pushy.
_____warms me: Jesus was patient with her.
other__

5) Salome has been compared to Peter. Some say she possessed many of the same qualities. There follows a list of qualities usually attributed to Peter. Which of these do you see in Salome? What others would you add as particularly applying to Salome?

_____direct _____ambitious _____practical _____outspoken _____devout _____intense _____impulsive _____enthusiastic _____independent _____loyal _____brash _____ energetic _____confident _____radical _____sensitive _____ capable   other__

Don't forget to make the research assignment for the next lesson on Deborah.

Chapter 8

Deborah
A Woman of Courage

Courage. The word can have many meanings, many connotations. This lesson is admittedly a flag-waver. It is meant to be an uplift, an inspiration to you. Take heart from the examples of women in history—like Deborah! *Recognize* your own courage. *Apply* this courage to your daily "battles" (or battles you may have been avoiding). And pray as you study.

At-Home Preparation

1) Read Judges 2:16–19; 4; 5. (Extended reading for leaders: Judges 2:11–3:4; 4; 5; Hebrews 11:32–34.)

2) Prepare your responses to "In the Lines" and "Between the Lines."

3) Read "About Deborah." Does this interpretation of the story and the people in the story change any of your former responses? You may disagree!

4) Complete the library research as assigned at the previous meeting. The rest of "You Are There" will be completed at the meeting.

Meeting Procedure

1) Compare and discuss responses to "In the Lines" and "Between the Lines" (25 minutes).

2) Discuss your reaction to the story, "About Deborah" (10 minutes).

3) Work as a group on "You Are There," including list of library findings, questions 1 to 3 (30 minutes).

4) Each woman will work separately on question 4 (10 minutes).

5) Close with brief volunteer prayers. Some may want to voice the prayers they have written in section 4 (10 minutes).

In the Lines

1) What moved God to send "judges" to Israel?

2) What was their function?

3) True or false: "The work of the judges was positive and lasting." Support your answer.

4) What background information does Scripture give about Deborah?
   a) Where did she live?
   b) Who was her husband?
   c) What was her role?

d) Describe one incident in her life.

5) Barak went along with Deborah's plan . . . on one condition. What was that condition?

6) Three prophecies made by Deborah were fulfilled in the story.

Prophecy   *Fulfilled*

4:7

4:7

4:9

Between the Lines

1) How do the "judges" described in Judges 2:16–23 differ from the modern definition of a judge?

2) Find the dictionary definition of *prophet(ess)*.

3) List other Bible women who were described as *prophetess*. (Terminology may be different in various translations, and your concordance may reveal still more than those listed here.) References given here are those which use the feminine form of the Hebrew (Old Testament) or Greek (New Testament) word for *prophet*.

Exodus 15:20   Nehemiah 6:14

2 Kings 22:14   Isaiah 8:3

2 Chronicles 34:22   Luke 2:36

Acts 21:9   1 Corinthians 11:5

4) Agree or disagree: "Barak questioned Deborah's instructions." Support your stand.

5) Why did Barak insist that Deborah accompany him into battle?

6) Who wrote the "song" of chapter 5? Support your answer.

7) This event is mentioned in the New Testament in Hebrews 11:32–34. Does the New Testament throw any new light on the event? Explain.

About Deborah

Deborah arrived suddenly on the stage of action during what is called in the history of Israel the "Period of the Judges"—a span of time between the death of Joshua (date uncertain, 1370 to 1210 B.C.) and the generation before the crowning of King Saul (about 1020 B.C.).

Deborah was fourth in a procession of thirteen judges. They were not judges in the sense of "adjudicators" but rather leaders called by God, endowed by God, and recognized and followed by the people of Israel.

Israel's history during this period revolves like a carousel: failure, oppression, repentance, leader, victory, relief, rest; failure, oppression . . . etc. Deborah is dropped into this procession—a leader called and endowed by God and empowered by him for a particular mission.

She lived and prophesied "under the palm of Deborah" (palm trees were rare in Palestine) in Mt. Ephraim, which was not a mountain but hill country, near Shiloh where the ark of God was kept. You may locate her home on a map of Palestine at a point twelve to fifteen miles northwest of the northern tip of the Dead Sea.

She might have sat quietly dispensing wisdom, but her people far to the north had for twenty years suffered a heavy oppression under the Canaanite king, Jabin. Jabin held high land, Hazor, north of the Lake of Chinnereth (Sea of Galilee). His fortress city cut across what was supposed to have been the territory of the Tribe of Naphtali.

The children of Israel "cried to the Lord, for he had nine hundred chariots of iron." And God heard and moved the heart of Deborah.

She might have resisted. The problems of Naphtali and their neighbors Zebulun were far removed from Deborah's palm tree in Ephraim. But she heard God's call and summoned Barak from his home in the capital of Naphtali, Kedesh.

Barak came. He hurried on the three- to four-day journey through hostile country, further attesting the respect commanded by this woman of Ephraim.

God had given explicit instructions to Deborah. Barak

was to gather ten thousand men—a small army in comparison to Sisera's (Jabin's general). Besides, Sisera had all those chariots! But Barak would have the advantage of knowing Sisera's battle plan. Sisera, Deborah said, was even then gathering his men near the River Kishon. Barak's strategy would be to rally his army on the heights of Mt. Tabor. (On your map, Tabor is just west of the southern tip of the Lake of Chinnereth; the River Kishon flows from the heights, westward to the Mediterranean Sea, entering the sea just north of the Carmel Peninsula.)

Far more than tactical advantage, Barak was promised the presence of God and sure victory.

Did he hesitate? Not exactly, but he did have a condition. "I'll go, if you go with me. Otherwise, no."

Perhaps Deborah expected his condition. She prepared at once to go into battle at the head of the army of Israel.

The battle, more fully described in the "Song of Deborah" in chapter 5, came off just as Deborah prophesied.

The news had leaked to General Sisera that Barak was mobilizing, so he speeded up his preparation, chariots and all. They spread across the plain—a formidable array to the small army on Mt. Tabor.

But Deborah was in touch with a higher Commander. When the time was exactly right, she gave the signal to attack, and Barak and Deborah and their army swept down the slopes.

There ensued what from the perspective of history is only one of the bloody battles fought on this, the Plain of Jezreel—except that the outcome of the battle was decided beforehand.

Heavy rains in the high country brought the River

Kishon to a sudden crest—a flash flood—which swept chariots, horses, and men toward the sea and left behind a residue of gummy mud which mired the wheels of the chariots that escaped the flood.

Josephus, the secular historian, adds a detail: "Sleet from the east blew into the faces of Sisera's men."

In any event, the army took flight with Barak and his men and Deborah hard behind. The slaughter was terrible. Sisera, however, escaped Barak, only to be murdered by a woman in whose tent he sought refuge and rest.

Details are not given, but apparently the destruction of Jabin's army opened the way for Barak to attack the fortress of Hazor itself with resulting complete victory.

The story ends with the words, "the land had rest forty years," but not before Deborah and Barak led in a triumphant victory song, extolling the power and care of God for his people.

You Are There

(Or in this instance, *"Deborah Is Here."*)

1) You will find here a list of words closely related to the word *courage*. Code each word: M—predominantly masculine; F—predominantly feminine. Some may be both.

____bravery		____guts
____valor		____fortitude
____heroism		____determination
____self-reliance		____confidence
____fearlessness		____resoluteness
____daring		____spunk
____nerve		____firmness

_____defiance   _____enterprise
_____aggressiveness   _____pluck
_____endurance   _____grit
_____prowess   _____devotion to duty
_____boldness   _____patience

   2) Go through the above list again and write a capital "D" beside each of the words which describes Deborah. What have you discovered? Did you learn something about Deborah? Be prepared to comment.

   3) The following list will have been divided and assigned the week before. Today you will all report your findings and fill in your chart. Your particular interest is what "battle" each woman was engaged in and what particular courage (the words in question 1 above may help) each exhibited. The list continues on page 74.

Abigail Adams   Rachel Carson
Jane Addams   Lydia Child
Marian Anderson   Shirley A. Chisholm
Susan B. Anthony   Margaret Corbin
Ida B. Wells Barnett   Dorothea Dix
Elizabeth Blackwell   Amelia Earhart
Emily Blackwell   Lucinda Foote
Harriet Stanton Blatch   Elizabeth Fry
Corrie ten Boom   Sarah M. Grimke
Catherine Booth   Julia Ward Howe
Nellie Bly   Lady Huntingdon
Antoinette L. Brown   Anne Hutchinson
Jane Campbell   Joan of Arc

Ann Judson
Fanny Kemble
Rose Hawthorne Lathrop
Ann Lee
Sybil Ludington
Margaret of Navarre
Margaret Mead
Helen Barret Montgomery
Bessie Smith Moore
Hannah More
Lucretia Mott
Florence Nightingale
Frances Perkins
Pocahontas
Pandita Ramabai
Jeannette Rankin

Esther Reed
Eleanor Roosevelt
Nellie Tayloe Ross
Letty M. Russell
Margaret Sanger
Hannah Whitall Smith
Elizabeth Cady Stanton
Lucy Stone
Harriet Beecher Stowe
Sojourner Truth
Harriet Tubman
Mercy Otis Warren
Lily Webb
Frances Willard
Mary Wollstonecraft

4) About myself:

a) Do I see courage in myself? Describe it—perhaps in the terms listed in question 1.

b) What is my current "battle"?

c) Am I avoiding a battle? Name it.

d) Do I need courage? Describe it.

e) Write a prayer, telling God about yourself and your needs.

5) Opportunity for sharing prayer.

Chapter 9

Shomer

(*The Woman at the Well*)
Finally, Someone Listened

The Bible does not name her, this Samaritan woman. So that we can feel more personal about her, we have given her a name which may have been a common one in her day. Her story is told in precise detail in John's Gospel. It seems fitting that John should be the one to recall and retell this story: John the sensitive, the intuitive, the "beloved" who walked so close to his Lord that he seemed almost to think his thoughts. The Holy Spirit led him to record this episode from the life of Christ for us.

At-Home Preparation

1) Read John 4; 7:37–39.

2) Prepare your responses to "In the Lines" and "Between the Lines."

3) Read "About Shomer."

4) Look over the "You Are There" questions, but reserve your work on them for the meeting.

Meeting Procedure

1) Discuss responses to "In the Lines" and "Between the Lines" (20 minutes).

2) "About Shomer" drew somewhat on cultural and historical facts of the time and place. Did this strengthen your understanding of the Bible account? (5 minutes.)

3) Work individually on responses to "You Are There," questions 1 to 4 (15 minutes).

4) If the group is larger than six, divide to discuss your responses (20 minutes).

5) Regroup to discuss question 5 (10 minutes).

6) Close in silent prayer. Let each woman think of someone who for one reason or another has been an "outcast" or considered "unreachable" and concentrate her prayers on asking God to change her own attitude and to direct her in reaching this person with the love of Christ.

In the Lines

1) Trace the route of the journey of the disciples and Jesus on a map.

2) Why was Jesus alone at the well?

3) How was the woman's announcement about Jesus received in the town?

4) What to you was the greatest revelation which Jesus made to Shomer?

Between the Lines

1) I see in this woman:
____an amoral person
____a woman who sought after and enjoyed a promiscuous life
____a victim of circumstances
____a woman exploited
____a world-weary person
____an admirable person
____a blatant adulteress
other__

2) Was Shomer a religious woman? Support your answer by at least three observations from Scripture.

3) How do you feel about Shomer?
_____ pity ____disgust ____repugnance ____interest ____curiosity ____contempt ____censure ____compassion   other__

Why?

4) What characteristics do you see in her?

____intelligent ____argumentative ____friendly ____
coy ____respectful ____hungry ____lonely ____curious
____arrogant ____daring ____devout ____devious
____religious other__

5) What do you learn about Jesus in this encounter?

6) What, do you think, was his purpose in asking a favor of her?

7) Jesus brushed aside at least three social barriers in this conversation. What were they?

8) Why is this episode given such prominence in the Gospel? Many other stories were not told (see John 21:25).

About Shomer

John, in his Gospel, calls her "a woman of Samaria," and in that brief description he has a world of meaning. As a Samaritan she was traditionally hated—and what is more, despised—by the Jews. The Samaritans' polyglomerate ancestry (although admittedly sharing some of the same forebears), their corruption of Jewish religion (even worse, they actually set up a rival religion), their history of nose-thumbing at the Jewish hierarchy—resulted in a hatred that was returned in kind.

Not only was Samaria an inhospitable country; it could be dangerous to a traveling Jew. The Jews demonstrated their repulsion in renaming the historic and sacred Shechem, the site of Jacob's well now polluted by Samaritan hands, as "Sychar": "drunkenness."

As a woman, Shomer was supposed to be incapable of intelligent conversation, particularly on a religious subject. Speaking with her was not only an undignified waste of time for a man but improper and endangering to a man's reputation.

Added to this, the account in John implies that the woman whom Jesus met at the well near Sychar was of questionable character: proper housewives joined the cooler, early morning and evening troop to the well, mingling with friends, sharing village gossip.

Jesus's insight also told him that she had had five husbands and was not married to the man she now lived with—which may mean a lot of things. Maybe her husbands had died. Divorce is more likely and in the Jewish tradition (which the Samaritans kept in part) it was, for a man, a simple procedure. He could conceivably divorce his wife if she consistently burned his food. A more common cause was the failure to bear children. Adultery was a sure reason.

We can only speculate on the cause for her many marriages. Whatever, unless a woman had an income-producing skill, she had little recourse except to seek the questionable protection of another man.

We don't know—but Christ did, and the woman knew he did.

Knowing that he knew did not threaten her or drive her away but filled her with excitement and expectation.

Still, she countered with questions meant to be argumentative and theological—a bait Christ refused to rise to.

How gently he led her! He talked to her politely. He listened respectfully, just as if she *was* somebody! And this kind stranger probed more deeply into who she really was than all the rebukes and insults that others had cast her way.

So much so that when he said, "I am the Christ, the Messiah," she was ready to believe him. In her excitement she hadn't time to carry her waterpots. Hurrying back to the town, she ignored social barriers; she told the men of the town, "Come! See him for yourself!" And they listened.

Nothing convinces like conviction. She was *so sure.* And Jesus, seeing "the fields ready for harvesting," stayed to confirm her ministry.

You Are There

1) You live next door to Shomer. You run out of water at midday, and are just stepping out of your door with your waterpot when you see Shomer leave her house with hers. What would you do, and why?

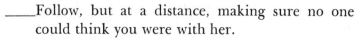

___Quickly duck out of sight and wait until she returned.

___Follow, but at a distance, making sure no one could think you were with her.

_____Call to her to wait for you, and walk with her.

2) Shomer comes running into town with her news. "Come see a man who told me everything I've ever done. Could he be the Messiah?" How would you respond? Why? (Note, however, it was the *men* she told.)

3) Shomer's modern counterpart—we'll call her Jane —lives just down the street from you. How would she have to change to be acceptable in your neighborhood? Or would a change in her lifestyle and behavior affect her standing?

4) Think about Jane again, only this time it isn't your neighborhood, but your Bible study group who are considering their relationship to her. Is there a difference? Why? Why not?

5) Someone has analyzed Jesus' method of reaching the woman of Samaria. Find the place in the text which illustrates these points. Compare Jesus' method—or more

particularly, his attitudes—with your own. How can he teach you?

a) He was courteous and respectful—so much so that she, who could spot a phony if anybody could, believed him to be sincere.

b) He opened the conversation with an item of common interest.

c) He asked her to do him a favor—placing himself somewhat in her obligation and making her feel good about herself.

d) He talked positively. About the "living water," for instance.

e) He did not rebuke her. Instead, she saw *herself* more clearly through him.

f) He refused to become involved in religious argument.

g) At the appropriate moment, he made a vital remark: "I am the Messiah."

Chapter 10

Rahab

A Day Changed Her Life

Rahab's story is a brief one. The wonder is that it is included at all. A Canaanite? An idolater? A harlot? And more embarrassingly, she became a forebear of King David! Yet, the account of her courage, ingenuity, and faith is necessary to an understanding of the Israelites' first success in the conquest of Canaan. And she so impressed the New Testament writers, fifteen hundred years later, that in both the Epistle to the Hebrews and in the Epistle of James, Rahab is held up as an example. She is immortal because she faced a crisis with courage and through faith moved in a new direction. Knowing Rahab may help you.

At-Home Preparation

1) Read Joshua 2:1–22; 6:15–17, 22–26; Hebrews 11:31; James 2:25. (Extended reading for leaders: Joshua 1, 2, 5, 6; Matthew 1:5; 21:31–32; John 8:1–11; Hebrews 11:31; James 2:25.)

2) Prepare your responses to "In the Lines" and "Between the Lines."

3) Read "About Rahab." Does the story surprise you?

4) Save your work on "You Are There" for group participation. Question 4 is for consideration at home.

Meeting Procedure

1) Compare and discuss responses to "In the Lines" and "Between the Lines," questions 1 and 2 (15 minutes).

2) Discuss the story, "About Rahab" (5 minutes).

3) Compare your charts for question 3: "What She Was"; "What She Became" (10 minutes).

4) If the group is larger than six, divide for the "You Are There" portion; emphasize your discussion of question 3 (25 minutes). Hold question 4 for thinking about at home.

5) Regroup for discussion: How has this lesson helped me in understanding my own decision points—past and future? Pray for members of the group, their family or friends, now involved in decision (15 minutes).

In the Lines

1) Joshua was at long last leading the people of Israel to the border of the Promised Land. What was his first target city?

2) What was his first step in preparing to take the city?

3) Why did the spies proceed no farther than Rahab's house?

4) What promise did she extract from them?

5) What two miracles particularly convinced the people of Jericho that resistance was futile?

6) Describe how Joshua kept the promise of his spies to Rahab.

Between the Lines

1) Considering Rahab's profession, does her request of the spies for the safety of her family surprise you? Why? Why not?

2) What about the story tells you that Rahab was: courageous?

industrious?

resourceful?

loyal?

loving?

intelligent?

believing?

practical?

trusting?

responsible?

3) Complete this chart:

Rahab, what she was		*Rahab, what she became*
profession: linen maker, innkeeper, harlot		
home: on the wall of Jericho	TIME OF DECISION	
national fidelity: Jericho		
religion: idolatry		
probable future: more of same		

About Rahab

She lived in a house built on the fortress wall of one of the oldest cities on earth. Near a gate, it was convenient for her business which was a combination of manufacturer of linen, innkeeper, and harlot. Rahab made a good living, for Jericho was a prosperous city and bustled with the passing of many caravans through this gateway from the east to the Mediterranean. Her goods and services were always in demand.

Lately, the city stirred with an ominous disquiet. From her vantage in the center of the city's commerce, Rahab received the full impact of the disturbance. For years the stories had sifted through about the nomad tribes, Semites, from Egypt. They swarmed like locusts—more than six hundred thousand fighting men. No king, no nation, could stand before them. Besides their overwhelming numbers, they were assisted by their god whom they called Yahweh—a god who forty years before had even rolled back the waters of the Red Sea to let them through.

Rahab pondered these stories as she bartered for flax, then soaked, pounded, spun, dyed, and wove it into luxurious cloth that brought traders to her door. Every story they told seemed to surpass the last. They would not talk so to their wives, but Rahab, businesswoman and harlot, shared their stories and their fears.

Now, they said, the Israelites were camped on the east side of the Jordan River, which was only five miles east of Jericho. The king of Jericho had of course sent spies, and in spite of attempts at secrecy the truth got out: the army was obviously preparing to cross. Their first target? Jericho, of course.

In the face of near panic the king organized parades and speeches to whip up the patriotic spirit of the people. Their walls were sound—twelve feet thick. Their gates were iron-clad. They had ample water from springs within the walls. Warehouses bulged with supplies of food and amunition. Their gods had received every supplication, every sacrifice. Jericho would not fall!

Nevertheless, some fled the city, preferring to risk arrest and death and to take their chances in the countryside. Most, though, relied on their defenses, their gods, and their own considerable experience in warfare.

What could Rahab, a woman, do? She had the extra responsibility of a large family—parents, plus brothers and sisters who had chosen a more respectable life, their families. Rahab felt as well a loyalty to her king and her city. And, like many others, she had this sense of outrage and anger that these strangers would dare to violate what had been theirs for millenniums.

While the rumors grew, Rahab's dilemma multiplied. Her loyalties, her faith in the idols worshiped by her fathers, her love of her city, her anger at the impending swarm of Israelites—and over against these a progressive conviction that these invader tribes were invincible because of the God they trusted. Yahweh fed them in the desert, led them in battle, confounded their enemies.

Eventually, everything she heard, all her heart said, told her that this was the true God. As much as she knew how, she prayed to Yahweh. He had no image, they said. There was no idol-figure for her to buy or make. He was a spirit. He was everywhere. Surely, then, he would hear her.

Some instinct told her that the two young men who sought lodging in her home were Israelites. They spoke her language haltingly, as many passing strangers did, but their accent was different. Their clothing was too new, their manner furtive.

Neither was she surprised when a messenger from the king appeared at her door to require the arrest of the two; the king's agents were everywhere.

For an instant her mind whirled. Her very life stood in jeopardy. If she were discovered harboring the spies . . . Yet, this was the opportunity she had prayed for.

She took firm hold on her courage. If Yahweh were the true God, he would help her now. The plan she had scarcely permitted herself to recognize rolled into action. The story that would mislead the searchers emerged smoothly. Now for the hiding place among the flax bundles . . .

In that moment of time, her loyalties, her faith, were decided.

And, being a practical woman and devoted to her family, she saw advantage as well in exacting a pledge of security from the spies she protected.

Once the searchers had left, the men Joshua had sent saw they need go no further: Rahab spoke for the whole city. "We have heard," she said, and described their exploits as well as they could have done. "Our hearts did melt, neither did there remain any more courage in any man because of you."

Aided by Rahab's ingenuity (she waited for night,

then let them down the outside of the wall with a rope) ,
the spies returned to the camp, jubilant in their discovery. "The people faint because of us! The city is ours!"

If there were any fearful before, they took courage
now.

And when Joshua heard of the spies' pledge to Rahab,
he took every precaution to see that it was honored.
The heavy linen rope, dyed scarlet: that was to be the
sign that protected her home. Weeks later, the spies
themselves were sent in to escort Rahab and her family
through the battle lines to a safe place outside the camp
of the Israelites (the camp was holy—no harlot was
permitted inside).

Rahab's faith changed her profession, and drew her
family as well into faith in the true God. They became
believers and part of the tribe.

Salmon, an Israelite of high rank, saw the courage and
genuine faith in this adopted daughter of Israel and
loved and married her. (Tradition says Salmon was one
of the spies.) God's approval is further attested in the
New Testament by her mention in Hebrews 11—one of
only two women in the gallery of the faithful. James, in
his manner, praised Rahab for her works.

You Are There

1) Why is this story included in the Bible narrative?
Many other details are passed over. Why not this one?

2) What if Rahab had decided to keep her loyalties

with her city and her gods? Imagine a brief sequel to the story.

3) Everyone in his or her lifetime stands at least once at a point of decision similar to Rahab's—a kind of "continental divide." There are lesser ones as well, but each is important in determining our future. Let each person of the group in turn describe at least one such decision-point. What factors figured in your decision? Were other persons influential? How did it affect your life direction? Can you imagine a "what-if?" similar to question 2? Have you crossed some decision points which you didn't recognize until they were past?

4) To think about this week:

a) Rahab is one of four women listed in the lineage of Christ (Matt. 1:1–17). The others are Tamar (Gen. 38); Ruth (Book of Ruth); Bathsheba (2 Sam. 11).

b) Read John 8:1–11; Matthew 21:31–32

Chapter 11

Michal

Helpless

Michal isn't exactly one of the heroines of the Bible. Her story is perhaps too earthy, too lacking in the elements that would make her an example and inspiration. Precisely because she *is* overlooked is why we bring her to your attention here. The scripture readings are unusually long, but you will find them interesting and all necessary reading if you are to know Michal, tragic wife of King David. (Note: in 2 Sam. 21:8, 9, more recent translations put Merab's name in place of Michal's—which is proper. The King James Version speaks of the five sons as "Michal's" because she became their foster mother.)

At-Home Preparation

1) Read 1 Samuel 14:49; 18:14–30; 19:9–17; 25:42–44; 2 Samuel 3:6–16; 6:12–23; 21:8, 9. (Extended reading for leaders: 1 Samuel 14:49; 16–31; 2 Samuel 1–7.)

2) Prepare your response to "In the Lines" and "Between the Lines."

3) Read "About Michal."

4) Prepare your responses to questions 1 to 4 in "You Are There."

5) "You Are There," questions 5 to 8 will be completed during the meeting.

Meeting Procedure

1) Compare responses to "In the Lines" and "Between the Lines" (15 minutes).

2) Discuss your reaction to "About Michal" (10 minutes).

3) Discuss your responses to "You Are There," questions 1 to 4 (10 minutes).

4) If the group is larger than six, divide to complete and discuss "You Are There," questions 5 to 8 (30 minutes).

5) Regroup to share thoughts on question 8. Close with a time of personal prayer, then recite the "Serenity Prayer" together (10 minutes).

In the Lines

1) Name the children of Saul, first king of Israel.

2) Whom did Saul first promise to David as his wife? Why was she denied him? What advantage did Saul see in Michal's love for David?

3) What do you understand the relationship between King Saul and David to be?

4) How did Michal save her husband, David's, life?

5) When Abner, commander-in-chief of Saul's army, defected to David's side of the conflict, what was David's first request of him?

6) What event brought a climax to the deteriorating relationship between Michal and David?

7) With what tragic event does Michal's story end?

Between the Lines

1) How would you describe David's attitude when he was offered Saul's daughters?

2) It's hard to overlook the savagery of the day and the unfeeling bartering of women, daughters and wives, and still see the story beyond it all. How do you feel about the violence and personal cruelty you read in this account? Do you find these attitudes hard to reconcile with the high position of Saul and David, and especially with David's superior image? How do you explain it to yourself?

3) Michal's ruse in helping David escape betrays the presence of idols in the king's house. How do you see this fact as relating to Michal's later reaction to David's celebration of the return of the ark?

4) David was in hiding for fourteen years. Describe Michal's adjustment during that period. Do you think Michal and David took up right where they left off fourteen years before? Why or why not?

5) Why was the return of the ark so important? What several factors brought on Michal's "despising" of David's "undignified exhibition"?

6) What does 2 Samuel 6:23 imply?

7) Describe briefly the facts of Michal's life from this time on. From what you know about her, what may have been her emotional state? List factors which contributed.

About Michal

She loved him. Who could resist this handsome, ruddy hero, the idol of Israel? At first even King Saul, Michal's father, had loved David (1 Sam. 16:21–23). He spent a lot of time about the king's home, and her brother Jonathan was his closest companion.

But as the younger of the king's daughters, it was to be expected that Michal's older sister, Merab, would be offered David as a prize for his exploits in battle. (Did Michal suspect that Saul, already burning with jealousy against David, was using Merab?)

But time passed, and her father, unpredictable and subject to drastic changes in mood, gave Merab to Adriel. Michal had reason to hope again—not realizing that she was but another pawn in her father's hands.

Saul never expected to fulfill his promise to David: the qualifying task he imposed in lieu of dowry would surely finish David off, he hoped.

Could it have been that David loved Michal, too? His enthusiastic claim would seem to say so.

Their early months together might have been idyllic except that more and more the specter of Saul's jealousy and hate threatened David. When Michal noticed an unusual number of Saul's men, his closest and most loyal, slipping about in the shadows near their home, she knew her father meant the worst. Her love led her to defy even the king and her quick thinking allowed David to escape. She had no way of knowing that fourteen years would pass before she would see him again.

Fourteen years. At first there was continual tension between Michal and her father because of her betrayal. Then worry over David as news reached her of his life in exile. Loneliness. She heard of his marriage to Abigail and to Ahinoam, and he seemed even further from her. About that time Saul gave her to Phalti of Gallim.

She heard as from another world that the tide of the conflict had turned in David's favor, that he had taken still more wives. The brief period of their life and love faded—until one day messengers from Ishbosheth, her one remaining brother, arrived to take her back to David.

What prompted David's demand? His continued love for her? His insistence on reclaiming his rightful property? The symbolic complete victory over the house of Saul which reunion with Michal symbolized?

Certain it was that their relationship was not the same. Too much had happened in the intervening years. Did Michal retain the idols she had kept in her father's house? Was her lack of faith in the living God the reason for her disdain at the sight of David leading the celebration dance as the ark of God was restored? Or had her love so declined, was her grief at being torn from a man who loved her still so fresh that everything about David displeased her?

Her sentence was instant and terrible. For the rest of her life she was only tolerated in the house of David. Other wives shared David's love, bore him children, and so were honored. Michal never again approached the king's chambers.

When her sister died, Michal invested her childless, loveless life in raising Merab's five sons. But even they were wrested from her and killed.

You Are There

1) What to you is the most beautiful thing about Michal's story?

The most painful?

The most disturbing?

2) You are Michal's friend—one of the few she confides in during the long, lonely years of her isolation in King David's palace. What questions would you like to ask of her to fill in the story of her life?

3) Note: Only three times did Michal assert herself

in action: she saved David's life, she ridiculed him for his religious dance, she raised her sister's sons. From these three assertive acts, how do you "read" her?

4) In all else, as recorded, her life was passive. List the events where she was helplessly acted upon:

5) Try to be Michal, as you perceive her to be: put yourself in her time and place, conditioned to be the property of her father or husband. How would you feel about the events you listed in question 4? How would you want to react to them?

6) We have described Michal as "helpless." Knowing her story, do you find that description true? If not, what could she have done to change the tragedy of her life?

7) When your will meets an insurmountable barrier, how do you handle the impasse? (Explore your unconscious as well as your conscious!)
____act the martyr ____deceive ____coax ____bribe

____cry ____praise the Lord anyway ____scheme
____override ____wait ____back off and reexamine
____be coy ____get a headache ____cheat a little
____talk louder ____demand your rights ____pray
for grace ____try another approach ____pray for
change ____try for compromise ____pout ____nag
____leave it to God   other__

If your answer is qualified by "it depends," invent some
situations and explore your different approaches.

8) The "Serenity Prayer" has become so common as
to be almost trite, but it is worth examining here:
   "O God grant me serenity to accept the things I
   cannot change, courage to change the things I can,
   and wisdom to know the difference."
How do you discern between what can be changed and
what cannot be changed?

Chapter 12

Miriam
A Woman Displaced

Miriam's ascent to leadership among the Hebrews was slow, hard-earned; her fall, like a burned-out rocket. You may have mixed feelings about Miriam's displacement. Did she deserve this disgrace? It's all right to feel ambivalent on this point—particularly if your self-searching leads you to explore your attitudes about your own or others' displacement and, more particularly, how in such circumstances you can express the love of Christ—to yourself, as well as to others.

At-Home Preparation

1) Read Exodus 1:7–2:10; 15:1–22; Numbers 12:1–16; 20:1; 26:58, 59; Micah 6:4. (Extended reading for leaders, add Exodus 14:1–15:22; Hebrews 11:23–29.)

2) Prepare your responses to "In the Lines" and "Between the Lines."

3) Read "About Miriam." Did you learn anything new? Is there some part of the story you want to check on?

4) "You Are There" will be completed at the meeting.

Meeting Procedures

1) Compare and discuss your responses to "In the Lines" and "Between the Lines" (20 minutes).

2) Discuss your reaction to the story, "About Miriam" (5 minutes).

3) Read Numbers 12:1–16. Make it a drama. Assign actors for Miriam, Aaron, God, Moses, and a narrator to read explanatory and connecting passages. Miriam has a long silence; mime her reactions (10 minutes).

4) Work individually on question 1, "You Are There." Write your responses, then share them with others in the group (10 minutes).

5) Discuss question 2 (5 minutes).

6) Work individually on question 3 (5 minutes). Discuss.

7) Work individually on question 4, then as the leader keeps score, tally your responses—so many votes for each item on the list or for others you have added. Discuss the results of your ballot (20 minutes).

8) Each person will work individually on question 5, closing in private, silent prayer (20 minutes).

9) Assign one class member to research question 2 from "Meeting Procedure," next lesson on Delilah. Suggested resource: church or public library, Bible encyclopedia, Bible geography.

In the Lines

1) From other references, we know the "sister" in Exodus 2:4–9 to be Miriam. Later we learn there was still another child. What was his name? Their parents' names?

Their tribe? Where did this opening drama take place?

2) How did the midwives deceive Pharaoh?

3) Why was the baby hidden?

4) Exodus 15:1–19 has been called the first recorded "national anthem." Who led the singing, dancing celebration? What was her title?

5) Aaron and Miriam had two specific complaints against Moses. Name them.

6) Did Miriam live to see the Promised Land?

Between the Lines

1) An unorganized, unconnected group of women saved the infant Moses' life. A careful reading of Exodus 1:7–2:10 will reveal six or seven names. List them.

2) The Bible says, and archeological finds and secular

history confirm, that the Hebrews, beginning with Jacob and his twelve sons, lived in Egypt well over four hundred years. Their knowledge of God, even when they arrived, had been minimal. How do you account for the "God-fearing" among the Hebrews of this story? (Also note Heb. 11:23–24.)

3) Miriam was probably about seven years old when she was assigned to watch the river bank. How do you "read" her in comparison with seven-year-olds that you know?

4) From the account in Exodus 12, what prompted Miriam and Aaron's accusations against Moses (read between the lines)? Why did God regard these accusations as such a serious offense?

5) Why was Miriam punished while Aaron received no punishment?

6) Note the reaction of Miriam's brothers (Num. 12:10–13). What does this tell you about their family relationship?

7) Miriam has one scriptural monument, written some seven hundred years later. Read Micah 6:4 and understand it.

About Miriam

A little girl ran barefoot beside her mother in the cool dark of the almost-morning. Her mother hugged close to her a kind of "boat" she had made from papyrus reed, lined with clay, waterproofed with pitch; in it lay a three-month-old baby boy, Miriam's brother.

Quiet. Above all, they must be quiet. To be discovered by the Egyptian guards would mean instant death.

For a girl of seven, Miriam had seen a lot of death. Boy babies torn from their mothers' arms. Slaves beaten to death. Neighbors dying from the plagues which swept through their hot, close-crowded villages. Death. Toil. Fear. Want. She knew them all.

The account of her watch by the riverside and her courageous, quick-thinking action was probably the first Bible story you learned as a child. From the vantage of adulthood you can appreciate the maturity and responsibility exhibited by this remarkable little girl.

Then she drops out of sight. Her brother, Moses, grew up as the beloved foster son of the princess and heir to the throne of Pharaoh. He wore the finest of linen, wide jeweled collars, and the elaborate headdresses reserved for the elite. He sat at tables heaped with food while the soothing music of harp, lute, and flute kept the diners in good spirits, or dancing girls were called to amuse their guests.

He studied, learning all the accumulated wisdom of Egypt: astrology, writing, accounts, warfare, art, architecture. He had access to the finest university and library in the world.

Miriam may have glimpsed him from time to time, this prince of Egypt. Did she resent his prosperity? Or did she watch him expectantly, knowing in her heart that one day he would return to his people? Their mother had been with him for seven years—long enough to be sure he knew about his roots. He knew it was his people whom he heard groaning and crying, laboring in the unbearable heat of the desert while he walked the cool cloisters of the palace and university.

He must remember!

Meanwhile, in the walled, adobe villages, ringed by guards, stinking with crowding, Miriam and Aaron achieved their own level of potential. Aaron became known as an eloquent speaker—Miriam a recognized leader, a singer of songs, a prophetess.

During the heat of the day they bore their share of labor in the stone quarries or the irrigated fields of the Nile Delta. They lived by the Egyptian seasons, as their people had done for more than four hundred years. Every now and then there was a feast day celebrating the birthday of one of the Egyptian gods or perhaps a thanks to the gods for the flood or the harvest. On such days the Hebrews would be issued an extra portion of food—even meat.

Aaron married and had three sons. Scripture is silent about Miriam, but the historian Josephus says she married Hur, a man who later became one of Moses' most

trusted leaders (Exod. 17:10–12), and was the grandmother of the talented architect, Bezaleel (Exod.
31:1–11).

How had her people maintained their tenuous faith
in Jehovah? We know they absorbed Egyptian culture.
Before the pharaohs "who knew not Joseph" came to
power (that is, under the Hyksos kings, who were in fact
distant kinsmen of the Hebrews), they had learned writing, the beginnings of science and engineering, the use
of metal, and the advantages of law in an organized society. They adopted the table and the chair from the
Egyptians; they learned to like Egyptian food. The architecture of the Egyptians was to follow them even to the
construction of their public buildings in Palestine, and
David's poetry would closely resemble that of Egypt.

They copied the Egyptians' family life—the nuclear
family—which was far different from the roaming tribal
life and multiple wives and concubines their ancestors
had known.

Against one Egyptian influence they held out stoutly:
the Egyptian gods. Egypt was a land of many gods—
changing with the whim of their rulers—but chiefly the
sun god who was represented by the pharaoh who was
himself a god.

Added to the Egyptian religious pressure was the
presence among them of other Semites—Canaanites and
Amorites—whose idolatrous religion bore no resemblance to that of Abraham.

And they had no scriptures—no written word from
their God.

How did they keep their faith?

They kept it through the perseverance of the faithful like Amram and Jochebed who so saturated their children with faith in the true God that Moses, though separated from his family, could never forget his God. And Aaron and Miriam rose head and shoulders above the tens of thousands of their kinsmen.

Came Moses' declaration of his loyalty, the years of waiting, and his return in the full strength of his manhood, radiant with the vision and call of God. The three were reunited.

Miriam is not mentioned in the drama of the plagues when Moses and Aaron called on Pharaoh again and again. But knowing her, before and after, we may assume her able leadership in organizing her people to leave Egypt, in encouraging their faith in God and in the leaders he had appointed. On the safe side of the Red Sea, the women followed Miriam in the celebration dance and song. A "prophetess" she was, and what a mighty trio of leaders (Mic. 6:4) !

The trials of the desert journey took their toll of morale and singleness of purpose. Her brother Aaron lost control while the multitude camped at Sinai waiting for Moses' return (Exod. 32). And soon after leaving Sinai, Aaron and Miriam, perhaps overly aware of their prominence and jealous of Moses' superiority, murmured against him. God responded in a flash of fury.

It was of supreme importance that the people recognize Moses' position and authority. God must exhibit dramatically his anger at their offense. Their punishment? Miriam was covered with the most dreaded of diseases, leprosy.

Aaron pleaded for her healing with Moses, who needed no such plea. He cried out to God, who lifted the plague after seven days' exile.

Was Miriam thus permanently demoted, disgraced? She is not heard from again, except that her death and burial are mentioned as occurring just before the Israelites reached the Promised Land.

You Are There

1) You and your neighbor from the next tent (we'll call her Sarah) pushed through the crowd to get close to the action near the tabernacle. You saw the whole scene. You watch Miriam stumble away, white with leprosy, the crowd parting widely. She disappears on the edge of the camp.

Sarah: She had it coming. She needed a good put-down.
You:

Sarah: Serve her right if she starved out there. Seven days, the Lord said. What about food and water? And she didn't have a blanket. But like I say, she had it coming.
You:

Sarah: I always say, you do right, God treats you right.
You:

2) Miriam was displaced from a position of respect, prominence, and leadership. Other "displacements," too,

can hurt. For a child, it could be the arrival of a new baby. For a teenager, a better bass comes along to sing in the quartet, and he's out. Name some adult displacements and tell why they hurt.

3) Check some of the following as what you feel might be—or has been—your reaction to displacement:
____anger ____guilt ____depression ____"get even" ____rebellion ____resignation ____blame someone else ____panic ____hurt ____repentance ____shame other__

4) What, in our day, in your circle of friends, puts a woman "out"—makes her unacceptable, out of status, lose respectability?
____selfishness ____wearing short-shorts to market ____hatred ____unruly children ____greed ____homosexuality ____pride ____sloppy housekeeping ____malicious gossip ____being pregnant and unmarried ____anger ____"running down" the preacher ____divorce ____hate ____having an "affair" ____religious "liberalism" other__

5) To survive a crisis—in the context of our conversation today, "displacement"—everyone needs a redemptive person. Someone to stand by, to rebuild a shattered ego, to restore confidence, assure acceptance—in short, to do what Christ would do. Invent a woman who

has suffered displacement for one of the reasons listed above. How would you go about being "redemptive" to that woman?

Maybe you didn't have to "invent" her: you know her. Well?

Don't forget to make the research assignment for the next lesson.

Chapter 13

Delilah

Manipulator

We really know so little about Delilah. Her name in history is synonymous with "villainess"—yet one so fascinating as to call out the talents of poets, composers of music, painters, and movie-makers. So she commands our attention today, this mysterious woman who wielded the only power she had, that of being a woman, to the downfall of one of God's chosen. Her tactic? It holds an uncomfortable resemblance to the dynamics of life around us day by day. We call it "manipulation."

At-Home Preparation

1) Read Judges 16:14–31. (Extended reading for leaders, Judges 13–16.)

2) Review from "About Deborah" the cycles of Israel's history during the period of the Judges, the function and definition of a judge.

3) Prepare your responses to "In the Lines" and "Between the Lines."

4) Read "About Delilah."

5) Look over "You Are There," but hold your responses until the group meeting.

Meeting Procedure

1) Compare your responses to "In the Lines" and "Between the Lines" (10 minutes).

2) Hear the report of the person assigned to research about the Philistines: their origin, territory, major cities, government, culture, skills, religion, relationship to patriarchs (Abraham and Isaac, Gen. 20:2–18; 21:22–32; 26:1–22), relationship to the Hebrew tribes in Palestine (10 minutes).

3) Discuss your reaction to the story, "About Delilah" (10 minutes).

4) If the group is larger than six, divide for work and discussion of "You Are There" (30 minutes).

5) Close with prayer in each group (5 minutes).

6) Assign portions of "Queen of Sheba," "You Are There," question 3, for the next meeting.

In the Lines

1) Describe the circumstances of Samson's birth.

2) Who was Samson's wife? What was her origin? How did this marriage end?

3) Samson was named a "judge over Israel." How did he arrive this prominence?

4) Describe Samson's second recorded amorous episode.

5) What persuaded Delilah to betray Samson?

6) How did she accomplish this?

Between the Lines

1) What does the casual tone of Judges 16:1 tell you about Samson's sexual habits?

2) Besides producing Samson, his parents are incidental but continuous in the story, down to the last sad line in 16:21. How do you see them? How do you feel about them?

3) How did Samson's feelings for Delilah differ from his feelings for other women he had known? Support your answer (read between the lines!).

4) Imagine Delilah's reaction when she first knew Samson was interested in her.

5) Look up dictionary definitions of *manipulate*.

About Delilah

We are not even sure she was a Philistine—this woman of Sorek who was to destroy the hopes of a generation of Israelites. She may have been an Israelite turned traitor because of the bribe offered her by the lords of the Philistines. To any woman of that day, eleven hundred pieces of silver (estimated at $3,500) was an enormous amount. Maybe it spelled freedom for her. A new life.

But first, before the story could begin, Samson fell in love with Delilah. Samson, the local judge of Israel. Handsome. Dynamic. Incredibly strong he was, and without a doubt his God was with him.

Considering the choice of sexual partners available to him, Delilah must have been one outstanding woman. Fascinating. A woman of exotic beauty. A woman so skilled in the essential art of man-pleasing that even the virile, assertive, spoiled Samson felt larger than life in her presence and returned to her again and again.

Was she a professional courtesan? Tradition says she was, but we can't be sure. Samson's repeated visits must have excited and flattered her.

Enter: the lords of the Philistines—five rulers of the five confederated cities of this coastal kingdom. For one hundred years they had kept the Israelites of the area in subjection. Joshua's arrival with the horde of Israelites had really been little threat to the deeply entrenched, highly organized Philistines. With their superior knowledge of iron smelting and forging, they had devised weapons far superior to the crude battle instruments of the Hebrews. What small area the tribes of Dan and Judah gained in their early enthusiasm was soon retaken. Dan, in particular, was contained in a small territory where the Philistines left no doubt as to who was in command.

Most important, the overlords kept the secret of iron from the Hebrews: if they would enjoy the use of superior agricultural implements—or even have them sharpened or repaired—the Hebrews must pay exorbitant prices to the Philistines.

But now and then, inspired by a tribal leader, the Danites would rise in a show of strength and unity. Samson was such a leader, and besides that, he possessed such personal strength and was so blessed by his God that even the Philistines' weapons were no match for him. The poet Milton described him, "weaponless himself, made arms ridiculous."

For nearly twenty years this man had plagued the Philistines. Now, hearing of his liaison with Delilah, they lost little time in approaching her. "Entice him," they said. "Find out where his strength lies, and how we can capture him."

It would not be fair to presume to know Delilah's reason for agreeing to the plan. But agree she did, and soon set about to arrange Samson's downfall with the only means at her command: her femininity.

In this art, she needed no teacher. She dressed in the finest, most seductive garments. Jewelry of gold and silver chimed and tinkled at her every movement. Perfumes of India met Samson at her door. Musicians played behind lavish tapestries. Tables were loaded with fruits and flowers.

His "secret" she had yet to learn; his weakness she already knew, and so she set about deliberately to press her advantage.

His resistance to her repeated questions, his "making a fool of her," only added to her determination. Her tactics did not change; they only intensified. She focused on his weakness. The marvel to the reader is how excessive was Samson's stupidity. Three times she cajoled him, three times she openly called, "The Philistines be upon you!" and stepped back to give them room.

Yet this man, already captivated by sex if not by ropes, kept coming back.

Eventually, of course, he gave in.

Where was Delilah when the Philistines rushed him, when Samson "shook himself," sure that his strength would return? Where was Delilah when, pitiful in his weakness, he screamed in agony as the Philistines gouged out his eyes and led him away in chains? Did she know remorse, or only satisfaction?

Was she with the crowd that assembled at Gaza to do honor to the god, Dagon? Surely by then she traveled among the elite. Did she see Samson's humiliation in being displayed like a circus side show? Did she know him well enough to shudder in apprehension, noting in a lull in the entertainment his deadly seriousness? Did she die with the thousands that fell in that crumpled heap of stone?

Scripture is silent on so much which would complete the story. But the essentials are there and we can read clearly that for whatever reason, with whatever emotion, Delilah manipulated Samson to his death and thus destroyed the hopes of his people for another one hundred years.

You Are There

1) From your combined definitions of *manipulation,* arrive at one which best describes Delilah's tactics.

2) If you were charged with such an assignment as Delilah's, how would you go about it? Or would you?

3) From the items listed below, mark with a T, "tools of manipulation"; with a P, "points of attack." Some may be both. Add others.

_____fear _____power _____weakness _____ignorance _____ need _____love _____desire to please _____pity _____authority _____sympathy _____insecurity _____loyalty _____ sex _____money   other__

4) From the following list of personal relationships, discuss several, and how manipulation might be employed to gain the ends of one or the other. Each pair listed may work in either direction.

manager, employees

students, teacher

elected official, public

patient, doctor

parent, child

tradesman, customer

wife, husband

5) Now that you think about it, have you used manipulation? Are you using it now? How do you feel about yourself? How do you feel about the person you have been or are manipulating?

6) Have you ever been manipulated? Did you know it when it was happening? How did you feel about it then? How did you react? How do you feel about it now?

7) What are some valid alternatives to manipulation?

Don't forget to make assignments for the next study on the Queen of Sheba.

Chapter 14

The Queen of Sheba
She Doubted

The Queen of Sheba was the original "show-me." Her visit to King Solomon of Israel was a PR trip, to be sure, but more than that, she had to see for herself that what had been a tiny, divided, beleaguered nation was now a world power and that its king possessed uncountable wealth and wisdom bordering on the divine. She doubted. Do Christians have doubts about God, his Word, his will, his working? How does God regard doubt?

At-Home Preparation

1) Read 1 Kings 10:1–13; Matthew 12:38–42. (Leaders read all the passages listed under "You Are There," question 3.)

2) Prepare your responses to "In the Lines" and "Between the Lines."

3) Read "About the Queen of Sheba."

4) Prepare your responses to "You Are There," questions 1 and 2, and the portion of question 3 assigned you at the last session.

5) "You Are There," questions 4 to 6 will be completed at the meeting.

Meeting Procedure

1) Compare responses to "In the Lines" and "Between the Lines" (10 minutes).

2) Discuss "About the Queen of Sheba" (10 minutes).

3) Discuss "You Are There," questions 1 and 2 (10 minutes).

4) Hear and discuss reports on "You Are There," question 3 (20 minutes).

5) If the group is larger than six, divide. Respond to questions 4 and 5 in small groups (15 minutes).

6) Each group will close by individual, silent reading of Matthew 27:39–46 and writing a personal prayer (10 minutes).

In the Lines

1) Find the present-day Yemen on the map. (Look on the far southern tip of Arabia.) This was the territory of ancient Sheba. By using the map scale, calculate about how far the queen and her caravan traveled to reach Jerusalem.

2) The queen came to test Solomon's wisdom. What did her testing prove?

3) She came to check out Solomon's reported wealth. What did she discover?

4) How did Solomon receive his guest?

Between the Lines

1) The Queen of Sheba could have sent ambassadors; it would have been an acceptable and more ordinary procedure. Give several reasons why you think she insisted on coming herself.

2) What spiritual or religious impression did she get at Solomon's court? Do you see any indication that her own faith was influenced by her visit?

3) From Matthew 12:42: What point was Jesus making in referring to the "Queen of the South" (Sheba)? (Note that this parallels Jesus' reference to Jonah.)

About the Queen of Sheba

The Sheba of ancient times (about 1000 B.C.) was unbelievably different from the Yemen of today, though their territory is about the same. The Sheba which the queen ruled was wealthy. Their advantageous position on the main route of world shipping produced a thriving trade in gold, frankincense, spices, and precious stones.

They also kept a flourishing slave trade, probably capturing their human commodity by raiding the eastern coast of nearby Africa.

In the day of the queen, a vast dam protected their major city, Seba, from mountain torrents and provided a reservoir against the dry season. So the country also maintained a healthy agriculture.

The Sabeans, residents of Sheba, descendants of Abraham and his second wife, Keturah, were distant cousins of the Israelites.

Today, Yemen is one of the lowest countries on the scale in terms of per capita wage, literacy, and life expectancy. Their religion is Islam. Their boast, ruins of times long past.

All of which points up the obvious power and acumen of the ancient rulers, including the queen who visited Solomon.

Probably the most dramatic of the strategic moves of her reign was this visit to Solomon. She could have sent ambassadors; other nations did. But such was her curiosity, her zest for adventure, her courage, and her compulsion to see for herself, that she undertook the dangerous, strenuous journey of some two months or more.

The wisdom and riches she saw in Solomon's court overwhelmed her; she was literally weak with a multitude of impressions.

Tradition says that during her long visit the queen and Solomon effected a sexual liaison, which is completely plausible. It might even have been an expected bit of diplomatic protocol in promoting relations between their countries.

The splendor of Solomon's kingdom was short-lived; in Jesus' day, as in ours, the visit of the Queen of the South symbolized the zenith of Israel's prestige and power.

So the unnamed queen, in her active curiosity, her honest doubt, and her courageous determination to seek the answers to her questions, created for us a legacy which we explore in our lesson today.

You Are There

1) If I had been the Queen of Sheba I would have

because I am

2) Do you consider yourself a "show-me" person, or are you naturally trusting? Give examples. Do you wish you were more trusting? More of a proof-seeker?

3) How does God feel about your doubting him? How does he respond to your questions? For your answer, hear the reports of members of the group as assigned at the last meeting. Each person will tell briefly: (a) who expressed doubt or questioned God; (b) what was his or her complaint or doubt; (c) how God responded (read on, if necessary). Note, too, that a "response" is not necessarily an "answer."

Genesis 18:9–15   Exodus 5:22–6:8
Exodus 3:11–17   Exodus 14:10–14

Psalm 77:7–9

Lamentations 5:20–22

Judges 6:11–24

Job 10:1–22

Job 30:15–23

Psalm 74:1–11

Matthew 11:2–6

Mark 4:35–41

Luke 24:1–12

Luke 24:13–35

John 20:11–18

John 20:24–29

4) With a renewed understanding of God's attitude toward your doubts, what would you ask him right now? (After writing your question, you may share with one another if you wish.)

5) Are you certain your question has an answer—even from God? How does "no answer" affect your faith and Christian life? Does "no answer" necessarily mean "no response"? Discuss.

6) Close in the small group according to "Meeting Procedure."

Chapter 15

Mary Magdalene

A Woman Healed

The Mary you meet here may at first seem strange. For too long "Magdalene" has been almost synonymous with "harlot." Centuries ago, some teacher with a flare for the dramatic but little sense of accurate biblical interpretation identified Mary of Magdala with another woman, a harlot, who found forgiveness and new life in Christ—an identification deplored and refuted by many generations of Bible scholars. But the dramatic story has stuck. Confusing the two women robs us of the particular meaning each was meant to have for us as we try to discover Christ through those who knew him best. In a study on the rescued harlot, our theme might have been "forgiveness." Mary emerges as one healed.

At-Home Preparation

1) Read Luke 8:1–3; John 19:25–20:18.
2) Prepare your responses to "In the Lines" and "Between the Lines."
3) Read "About Mary."

4) "You Are There" will be completed at the meeting.

Meeting Procedure

1) Compare responses to "In the Lines" and "Between the Lines" (10 minutes).

2) Discuss "About Mary." Did this interpretation add to your understanding of her? Did it change your concept of her (10 minutes)?

3) If the group is larger than six, divide for meditation and discussion of "You Are There" (30 minutes).

4) Regroup. Close by singing or reciting the hymn-poem found at the close of "You Are There."

In the Lines

1) What four facts about the Mary of our study can be learned from Luke 8:1-3?

2) We have heard of other followers who fled in terror when Jesus was arrested and executed. Who stayed by him?

3) Why was it important that Jesus' body be removed from the cross before Friday evening?

4) What clinical proof of Jesus' death does John offer?

5) What disciple is alluded to in John 20:2–9 but not named?

6) Verse 18 contains the last reference to Mary Magdalene in all of Scripture. What was her final word?

Between the Lines

1) Mary was one of the "set-free" women named by Luke. What had been her particular bondage? How would you describe her social and financial status?

2) Mary of Magdala was one of the few who endured the agony of staying near Jesus through his tortured death, and Matthew 27:61 notes that she lingered for his burial. What compelled Mary to participate in this agony and to defy the danger of association with Jesus?

3) In the quiet of your heart, live the scene on Calvary. What did it mean to Jesus to see Mary Magdalene there?

4) The two men who took charge of Christ's hasty

burial had been secret believers. Whom did they fear? Why did they now come out of hiding?

5) After finding the empty tomb, the disciples returned home: Mary lingered. Why?

6) Mary does not appear surprised when she sees the angels. Why?

7) How did Mary recognize the Lord?

About Mary Magdalene

Did she go seeking him? In her lucid moments—times even more tortured than when the spirits within drove her to insane acts and thoughts—did she see in this vagabond rabbi a hope of healing?

Or did he happen upon her on one of his many journeys between Tiberius and Capernaum? Was it in a crowd he noticed her—raucous, wild? Or did he find her alone in the shadows of suicidal despondency?

We don't know. The Gospel writers only describe what *had* happened: none of them describes the healing.

"Seven devils" had come out of her, the "seven" indicating the totality of her possession. Her symptoms, even among a myriad of persons possessed, were outstanding and memorable.

Maybe today her disorder would be described as an extreme form of mental illness. Maybe not. In more primitive societies even today demon possession is recognized as something quite different from mental disorder.

But to belabor this point when we cannot know the answer is to miss the point: Mary of Magdala was a tormented woman. Living was death for her and pain for all who loved her.

We have reason to think she was young and of a comfortably prosperous and respected family. How did her illness-possession show itself? In violent rage? In lewd exhibition? In attempts at suicide? In long periods of nonspeaking withdrawal? The "seven demons" set her apart from functioning, responsible society.

In the times between, the terrible tortured hours when the demons rested, how she must have cried for deliverance, praying to die decently and so rid her family of their humiliating burden.

But Jesus came. Invisible chains fell off. The beautiful shone through tranquil eyes. The rational spoke through a controlled voice. She smiled. She worked. She loved. And all around marveled at her healing. Most of all, Mary.

The miracle was greater than a resurrection. For the dead are not aware of their deadness. Mary suffered every moment of hers. And to the One who had brought such healing Mary turned for continuing light and strength.

She joined the band of women who followed Jesus and his disciples. She gave of her means. She cooked, washed, served.

And she listened. Only about the edges, of course, but she heard and witnessed the love and energy that flowed from this remarkable Teacher. She and the other women pass almost unnoticed—until the crisis. When their lives were on the line, when others forsook Jesus and fled to anonymity and safety, several of the women stayed by him, and Mary was one.

She agonized with him on the cross. She heard his, "It is finished," and saw the soldier pierce his side. She stayed close by as Joseph and Nicodemus received the limp body and watched as they wrapped him and laid him in Joseph's own tomb. She saw the huge stone rolled in place.

Only a person of unusual inner strength and poise could have endured such an emotional pounding as Mary subjected herself to. She and another woman were the last to leave . . .

. . . and the first to return to the tomb.

The Gospel accounts of events around the resurrection vary but they do not refute or conflict as much as they augment one another. Each author tells what most impressed him in those emotion-packed hours.

It would be John, of course, who remembered and recorded the poignant scene in the garden where the loving, heartbroken Mary Magdalene was the first to see the risen Lord.

In our last glimpse of this transformed woman, she bursts upon the confused, frightened disciples with the great, confirming news: "I have seen the Lord!"

You Are There

An experience in private meditation.

1) Have you felt at some time that you were *indeed* there—balanced on a precarious point between sanity and insanity?

2) What circumstances or life experience precipitated or surrounded this experience?

3) What was it like there, on that point?

4) What, or who, brought you back into the safety zone?

5) Do you dread other episodes?

6) Would it help you to know that the experience is a common one—especially for women and more especially for young mothers?

7) Would it help to be able to talk to someone about

the internal pressures, angers, and frustrations that may precipitate these crises? Would it help even to admit to yourself that they exist?

8) Someone has suggested that one's emotional state may be illustrated by a straight line—perfect sanity at one end, insanity at the other, with a "gray" or overlapping portion in the middle. Most of us live most of the time closer to the "sane" end. Now and then, in crisis or stress, we move toward the middle. This is a normal, expected experience, which nearly always contributes to growth and self-understanding. How does this illustration compare with the "peaks and valleys" picture:

a) in helping you right now?

b) as a source to draw upon when you need it?

9) Would it help to know that those who are most susceptible to emotional pain are also most capable of the joy and appreciation of life? That those who hurt can in turn be those who heal?

10) Having successfully come through such crises, are you sensitive to other women in crisis? Do you try to help? How?

11) By now you know the members of your group very well. You have shared many experiences and much personal probing. If you feel like talking to your group about your response to this time of meditation, lead the way: others may follow.

12) Close according to "Meeting Procedure."

> Just as I am—poor, wretched, blind;
> Sight, riches, healing of the mind,
> Yea, all I need in Thee to find,
> O Lamb of God, I come! I come!

Maggie Mason is a freelance writer and editor living in Topeka, Kansas, where she is also communications coordinator for Memorial Hospital. She has five daughters, all married, and fourteen grandchildren. In her 34 years as a minister's wife she did a lot of Bible study and teaching as well as speaking. She is a member of the Evangelical Covenant Church.